Demystifying the Manuscript:

Essays and Interviews
on Creating a Book of Poems

Edited by Susan Rich & Kelli Russell Agodon

Two Sylvias Press

Two Sylvias Press
PO Box 1524
Kingston, WA 98346
twosylviaspress@gmail.com

Cover Design: Kelli Russell Agodon
Book Design: Annette Spaulding-Convy
Cover Photo Credit: Tolga Tezcan

"To the Book" by W.S. Merwin appears in *Present Company* (2005, Copper Canyon Press) and is later included in *The Essential W.S. Merwin* (2017, Copper Canyon Press). Used by permission of the publisher.

Created with the belief that great writing is good for the world, Two Sylvias Press mixes modern technology, classic style, and literary intellect with an eco-friendly heart. We draw our inspiration from the poetic literary talent of Sylvia Plath and the editorial business sense of Sylvia Beach. We are an independent press dedicated to publishing the exceptional voices of writers.

For more information about Two Sylvias Press please visit:
www.twosylviaspress.com

First Edition. Created in the United States of America.

ISBN: 978-1-948767-18-7

Two Sylvias Press
www.twosylviaspress.com

This Book is Dedicated to Linda Pastan

(1932 - 2023)

*And each partial metaphor,
like a good investigator, searches
for its other half—the clue
that explains everything.*

from Linda Pastan's *The Collected Poems*, "Crimes"

To The Book

Go on then
in your own time
this is as far
as I will take you
I am leaving your words with you
as though they had been yours
all the time

of course you are not finished
how can you be finished
when the morning begins again
or the moon rises
even the words are not finished
though they may claim to be

never mind
I will not be
listening when they say
how you should be
different in some way
you will be able to tell them
that the fault was all mine

whoever I was
when I made you up

~W.S. Merwin

Table of Contents

II. Behind the Scenes: Thoughts from Editors

III. Moving Towards Publication
Once the Manuscript is Complete

IV. Resources and Ideas

Introduction

Book Creation is an Art

~Susan Rich & Kelli Russell Agodon

The book you hold in your hand is a vessel. It contains everything you will need to create your own book of poems. In these pages you will find helpful chapters that include information on how to order your manuscript, insider tips from a diverse group of poets, and interviews with poetry editors themselves.

We decided to put this book together while we were working on our recent collections of poems. We've led classes on "Demystifying the Manuscript" and oftentimes students would come up to us at the end of the workshop and ask for a resource with all the information we had shared. Over time we have realized that there is no single comprehensive resource for poets on preparing a poetry manuscript that explores all of the details of a book—ordering the collection, choosing sections / no sections, cover art, deciding on a title, and much more.

Please understand that there is no one "right way" to organize or create a poetry manuscript, but rather a wide variety of options. Jane Hirshfield says that there are very few things in this world that we can craft and control as much as our poetry collections. View this anthology as a toolkit for creating your book—maybe you have questions on how to order your collection or maybe this is your first volume of poetry—in either case, we hope this book gives you the tools you need as well as inspiration from other poets and editors who have walked this path before you.

As writers who have published a dozen books between us, we have worked to create a book that functions as a portable mentor. As poets ourselves, we know well the struggle and self-doubt that can appear while trying to shape a manuscript.

Sometimes as poets, we get lost in the "what ifs?" when working on our manuscript. Jeff Shotts, poetry editor at Graywolf Press tells us "Dare to sound like yourself and no other." Kelly Davio, cofounder of *Tahoma Literary Review* and former Eyewear Editor, states "What I'm looking for is a fresh approach."

Surprisingly, a book of poems is not only about the poems themselves. Over the course of many books, we discovered the importance of details: section titles (or symbols), quotes, manuscript titles, endnotes (or not to have endnotes), and how to keep going after the first, second, or third collection. We hope to share all the details that may have been overlooked.

May this literary toolkit offer you inspiration and the essential details needed as you put together your own manuscript.

Yours in book creation,

Susan & Kelli

One Size Does Not Fit All

~Susan Rich

Spread out before you across the living room floor lay islands of poems that you have painstakingly written. On a good day you feel extremely proud of your creations. You watch them fan out like pages for a primary school project—only you are much more interested in this work than anything you did in primary school.

One place to start organizing your manuscript is by taking a stack of notecards and writing the title of a poem at the top of each card. Under the title, you can write the first line of the poem and at the bottom of the card you can write the last line of the poem. This gives you an easy, portable way to sift through your poems and reshuffle them. Is the last line of one poem talking with the first line of another? In this way you can discover unusual juxtapositions of sound and sense. For example, I have one poem that ends with "a young girl/ who goes out, who doesn't lock the door" and that led me to place it next to a poem that begins "Get in, Omar says." Out one door and into another is a lyrical bridge that I might not have discovered without the note cards to help me.

So now what?

While there are books and workshops, certificates, and MFA programs to help you write better and better poems, the resources for ordering your poems into a manuscript are comparatively scarce. Perhaps you've looked for a "how-to guide" for organizing a manuscript or anything that might tell you what you need to know. That's where this collection of essays, interviews, and resources comes in.

One thing to remember: the same poems organized in a different way will result in a different book. In other words, one ordering might result in a collection about the death of your mother while another order will highlight the tension between international travel and creating a life closer to home. The same poems ordered differently create an entirely new narrative. Try out different orderings, write a list of new poems that could fill in the "gaps" should your book become built around a traditional chronology or a collage or even a history-based project. It is not unusual to write new poems to enhance your manuscript once you've decided on what structure you want to employ. It is not unusual to rip one order up and start again.

We want to introduce you to several strategies for putting *your* book together. *Your book.* There are very few things in the world that you have more control over than how you compile your collection of poems. Sure, there are trends to understand. For example, as we write this, there is a movement in book publishing towards skinny collections. Less poems in a manuscript means each one needs to be a showstopper. A good friend of ours just published her book with a mere forty-one poems. That is nearly as skinny as a poetry book can be and not be categorized as a chapbook. However, another poet we know was asked by her editor to add more poems to her manuscript. The publisher felt that readers would want more poems for their dollars. What works for one writer may not work for you. The secret is to explore all the available options.

Project Focused Collections

While there is usually a theme running through any collection, some books are more subject heavy than others. For example, Mary Jo Bang's *Elegy,* winner of the National Book Critics Circle Award for Poetry, is a series of poems written in the aftermath of her son's death. Every poem explores his life or her grief directly. On the one hand, a book so clearly "about" one subject might be an easier book for an editor to understand; however, it also runs the risk of repetition. How does grief take on a myriad of forms without becoming too oppressive, eventually losing its emotional power—no matter how compelling the topic? Bang solves this problem with the use of a careful chronology. The poems open with the policeman at the door, informing the speaker of her son's death. What follows is a year-long journey into surviving the loss of a child. We experience the speaker's seasons of grief as fall, winter, spring, and summer move past her. The chronology allows for a sense of movement; something that is strongly required as a counterpoint to the emotional stasis.

Another example of a project-focused collection is the beautiful first book by Valerie Wallace, *House of McQueen*. Here, Wallace explores her obsession with the British fashion designer, Alexander McQueen, who famously stated, "I want people to be afraid of the women I dress. I've seen a woman get nearly beaten to death by her husband. I know what misogyny is." Wallace employs a showcase of different invented forms to open up her topic. After the first section of the book, she leaves traditional biography behind and instead focuses on more universal questions of creation and design. For example, in the poem, "McQueen Self Portrait as Bestiary," each of the five sections focuses on a different animal (raven, snake, moth, jellyfish, hawk) speaking out as the persona of the designer. The book also includes extensive notes which allow a reader not familiar with Alexander McQueen to feel up to date on the facts of his life.

We suspect that not every book that is published on a specific theme or place started out that way. In fact, sometimes a book becomes known as a subject focused book when perhaps only a handful of poems speak directly to that theme. Carolyn Forché's second collection, *A Country Between Us,* is an excellent example. Mention this title to most poets and they quickly mention the El Salvadoran civil war of the 1980's. Yet, of the entire collection less than ten poems are focused on El Salvador. The power of these poems, which frontload the book, lends a cohesiveness to the work, and when the reader looks at a poem about a train ride, it is in the context of the key poems. In other words, not every poem has to be about your main topic. Let the work have room to expand outwards. Create spaces to breathe throughout the book.

Other collections and chapbooks include:

Dien Cai Dau by Yusef Komunyakaa
Still Life with Two Dead Peacocks and a Girl by Diane Seuss
Dime Store Alchemy by Charles Simic
In the Convent We Become Clouds by Annette Spaulding-Convy
The Wise and Foolish Builders by Alexandra Teague
Here, Bullet by Brian Turner

Historical Collections, a Subset of Project-Based Collections

There are, of course, as many poetry projects to imagine as there are galaxies in the sky, maybe more, but one very popular subgenre is that of the historical period collection. This could take the form of persona poems in the voices of 19th century Midwest women pioneers in traditional forms—sestinas sonnets, villanelles—as well as received forms (self-designed) such as in Katelynn Hibbard's stunning book, *Simples,* where the female body is the focus of the work in surprising and carefully researched ways.

Another example of the historical collection is *Bellocq's Ophelia* by former US Poet Laureate and Pulitzer Prize Winning author, Natasha Trethewey. Her book tells the "story" of a semi-fictional prostitute, Violet, who lived in Storyville, the red-light district of New Orleans. The cover photo shows the actual photograph of a turn-of-the-century biracial prostitute. Trethewey imagines the life of an educated woman who can find no other employment due to her race. At one point the (constructed) Violet meets the (real life) photographer, E.J. Bellocq, famous for taking photographs of prostitutes during their off hours: drinking coffee, washing clothes, hanging out in the kitchen with their friends.

Researching historical movements and people is guaranteed to bring your poems into a new realm. In other words, an obsession outside the self is another way to give your poems some fresh air. You are, of course, the author of these poems and so your life and aesthetic concerns will be showcased no matter what topic you write about, but in a historical collection, you can come at your concerns from a slightly different direction.

Braided Collections

If you have ever braided a child's hair, baked challah, or created a lanyard at sleepaway camp, you know the basic motion of taking three separate pieces of similar material and joining them together, one at a time. Sometimes this works for poems, too. Many of us do not write about only one subject. Life often overlaps: a new home, the death of a grandparent, and a child growing up can happen all at once, and often does. Your poems might focus on the life of a contemporary woman (or man) but that's still somewhat broad and as a collection could feel a bit fuzzy around the edges. Distinguishing 3-5 threads and braiding the work together brings cohesion to an otherwise diffuse group of poems. Sometimes, one of these threads takes precedence over the others, but the themes are still brought together into a cohesive whole by the juxtaposition of the individual poems.

One such collection is January Gill O'Neil's third book, *Rewilding*. *Rewilding* is an environmental term, which means restoring (an area of land) to its natural uncultivated state (used especially with reference to the reintroduction of species of wild animal that have been driven out or exterminated). O'Neil has stated in a couple of interviews that her intention here is to "rewild" her own life. The exquisite poems primarily examine the speaker's divorce, her children, the larger world, and a rewilding of the self. The titles of poems such as "First Sex After Divorce," "Mad Lib for Ella," "On Being Told I Look Like FLOTUS, New Year's Eve Party 2014," and "Tinder" give strong clues to the overarching themes. Each poem is a pitch-perfect piece of music and together, the book works like an album that you want to listen to over and over again.

Most books have at least some degree of braiding underneath their order. In today's poetry world, it is natural to write from one's direct experience and that means various threads of a life that somehow come together. Another advantage of braiding your work is that your poems don't have to compete against each other. For example, if you placed all your break-up poems side by side, the work would too easily be measured against itself, while if you placed a break-up poem next to a poem about your childhood home and that poem next to a poem focused on a pomegranate—your subjects can appear more surprising just by which poem they are placed next to.

Rick Barot's book, *Chord, is* another favorite collection of mine. In what appears seamless, Barot weaves together poems with subjects as varied as art ("Black Canvas," and "Looking at the Romans"), place ("Tacoma Lyric," and "Coach Starlight"), and politics ("After Whitman," "Darwish," and "Election Song"). More than anything else what brings this award-winning work together is the poet's voice. Voice is the author's style, the characteristics that make her writing distinct. The vocabulary, syntax, and sonic characteristics of the poems unite them just as much as the three subjects.

Other braided collections include:

The Tradition by Jericho Brown
The Book of What Stays by James Crews
Registers of Illuminated Villages by Tarifa Faizullah

Collaged or Hybrid Collections

In recent years, the poetry collection as a hybrid form has gained a good deal of currency. Lyric essays and poetic questionnaires are quite common these days as are prose poems, visual poems, and found poems. In fact, it seems what one thinks of as a poem is changing at lightning speed. Like a visual collage, creating a manuscript that includes lyric essays, found poems, prose poems, visual poems, letter poems—can offer the reader a more exciting read. As the poet building this book, the style allows you to "get at" your topic from multiple perspectives. Catherine Barnett's third book, *Human Hours* (Graywolf Press), is divided into four sections, each with a lyric essay that functions as a pillar for the book as a whole. Oliver de la Paz's book, *The Boy in the Labyrinth* (Akron Press), uses poems based on medical questionnaires as an organizing strategy.

Collaged / Hybrid Collections:

Toward Antarctica by Elizabeth Bradfield
Home Water, Home Land by Katy E. Ellis
Jane by Maggie Nelson
Citizen by Claudia Rankine
Brown by Kevin Young

Narrative Arc

The organization of a book of poems focused on a narrative follows the scaffolding of a traditional story: there's an introduction, complication, climax and falling action. In other words, the book might open with poems of the speaker's childhood, move on to a search for identity, climax as the speaker shifts into the role of wife and mother, and then finish with poems that show a renewed sense of potential. Aimee Nezhukumatathil's book, *Lucky Fish,* follows this convention. There is a strong comfort in presenting your book this way. People, both poets and non-poets, respond to the pull of narrative. Nothing fancy, just superb poems ordered in a way that tell a story: beginning, middle, and end.

Books that Employ Narrative Arcs:

Lucky Fish by Aimee Nezhukumatathil
Deaf Republic by Ilya Kaminsky
Human Hours by Catherine Barnett

Then There's the Blue Plate Special

The truth is that most books are comprised from a mix of these different approaches. A project-based collection may also have an emotional arc which adds more tension; a braided collection often tells a story, has a narrative arc.

How will you know which organizing strategy suits your book best? One writer suggests trying out at least three different ways before committing to one. Many poets we know invest in a spring binder, which can create a prototype of the book for you to use at readings, but more importantly, it lets you see exactly how your manuscript will look as a book. Print out three different orders and then ask a friend to take a look at each one. At some point (and it's different for every book), one order will instinctively start to feel complete. And as you write new poems you will inevitably need to prune the weaker poems out or rearrange what you have. This happens. It's part of the process—the frustration and the joy.

Journeying Through the Inner Pages

After you have chosen your strongest poems and finally ordered them according to a strategy that feels good to you (at least for the moment), well, you must be almost done and ready for book publication, right? Not exactly. Actually, there are more decisions and indecisions ahead. A myriad of considerations awaits you regarding the table of contents, including sections (or not), and using endnotes (or not). These aspects of your book are just as important as any individual poem. Robert Frost famously said, "If there are 24 poems in a book of poetry, the book itself is the 25th poem." We experience the individual poems differently when they are part of a larger work, which in the 21st century can include artwork, symbols, epigraphs, QR codes, and more.

Think of these choices as analogous to what a ceramicist must do once her bowl comes out of the kiln. She has her piece in-hand but now she's faced with more decisions regarding its color, the type of glaze (matte or high shine), and texture. These decisions go beyond the decorative and get at something much deeper. What does this pot represent?

In her essay, "Mighty Meta: The Language of Your Book as a Book," poet Sandra Beasley refers to these style decisions as the "mighty meta." But what does she mean by this? Beasley goes on to explain, [the meta] *indicates an enriching gesture that references the book's own conventions.* In other words, you can think of these elements as clues for your reader—looked at together they provide a map of your intentions which go beyond the individual poem. Here again is the color and glaze and the texture of your manuscript; the exterior appearance of your poetry which can give nuanced clues as to what is to come.

Sections, No Sections, or Something In-Between

Let's start with the question of whether to use sections in your book. In the structure that you chose, you may have already divided the poems into a narrative with a beginning, middle, and end. For a long time, it's been a customary default to use three sections in a book, perhaps adding in an extra one if the book includes a discrete portfolio of poems gathered on a certain subject—a group of ekphrastic poems, for example, or a small group of poems about a historical event.

Martha Silano, the author of five books of poems including *Gravity, Assist*, (Saturnalia Press), shares her section strategy, the one she has used in each book she's published:

I usually have three sections. I enjoy ending sections with a powerful close or hint of what's to come. I can't imagine sustaining a manuscript for 50+ pages without pauses—it gives the reader a break, too.

Silano's succinct answer is echoed by an entire generation of writers. Looking back at the last decade of poetry publications, the vast majority of books have employed the three-section option—a comfortable format that readers recognize and respond to. Think about attending a local theatre production or perhaps a play on Broadway—the audience needs an intermission. Maybe the time is spent grabbing a glass of wine or rereading the playbill or chatting with a friend about a favorite character or stage set or visiting (that lovely vintage place) the powder room. In other words, like theatrical intermissions, dividing your book of poems into three acts offers readers time to sit back and contemplate what they've read, perhaps reread a favorite poem, and to consider the meta nature of one section before moving on to the next poems.

Another dear poet friend adds:

I love section titles! Yes, my current manuscript has them. I do think a book without sections has to do a lot of work to keep my attention. When I added sections to my second book, it got accepted soon after. I don't think I was giving the reader enough room to pause.

However, the book that wins the trophy for the most creative and extensive use of sections goes to Diane Seuss's fourth collection, *Still Life with Two Dead Peacocks and a Girl* (Graywolf Press). The collection contains thirteen sections, each one demarcated with a segment of Rembrandt's painting from which the book takes its name. One section begins with the image of a bowl of fruit, the next with the disturbing legs and feet of a peacock, and the next with a large pool of blood. Some sections offer a location for one long poem, such as "Walmart Parking Lot," while another section offers a portfolio of seven "Self Portraits" with different people and places. In total the book holds over one hundred pages of poems covering a variety of interconnecting subjects from the strangeness of Dutch Masters to the death of the narrator's father, from the re-imagined Emily Dickinson to a persona poem from Andy Warhol. Without multiple sections created in a variety of ways, this book might have seemed unwieldy instead of depicting a multi-faceted mirror of contemporary life. This museum of a world benefits from the orderliness that discreet sections provide.

In Jenny Xie's, *Eye Level,* her first book and Finalist for the National Book Award, she has discovered how to have it both ways—sections and no sections. This makes sense given her double focus on traveling far from home, and at the same time, searching for where she belongs. Even the title, *Eye Level,* is intended as a palindrome. The sections of the book are neither named nor numbered, instead each of the four parts are marked with a dot and field of white space in the table of contents while within the internal pages, each section is depicted with one vanishing line, drawn like a horizon—at exactly eye level. The minimalism of the section design matches beautifully with the content of the book.

The effect offers the reader brief pauses within this set of forty poems. The first section introduces the reader to a speaker who is traveling through Phnom Penh and Corfu. These poems lead to a central inquiry of the book in terms of cultural displacement and, in turn, a philosophical reckoning with the self. What is important here in terms of the book's architecture is how the sections reinforce the book's message with a subtle and appropriate metaphor.

Don't Call Us Dead (Graywolf Press), the second full-length collection by Danez Smith, Finalist for the National Book Award and Winner of the Forward Prize for Poetry, also opts for a minimalist approach to the "mighty meta." In the table of contents, the four sections are divided with no titles or symbols but a single line of white space. Within the book's pages, the sections are denoted with the symbol of three colons :::, which the Urban Dictionary compares to a traditional ellipsis … only this ::: indicates a more dramatic pause. As with *Eye Level,* the meta narrative of content markers brilliantly mirrors the collection's content.

Finally, the section markers disappear entirely in Claudia Castro Luna's first full-length collection, *Killing Marias: A Poem for Multiple Voices*. There are no sections in either the table of contents or the interior pages, and the effect is unexpectedly powerful as the reader is compelled to read the entire book, 45 one-page lyric poems (many of the poems rendered in only a few lines) in one sitting. The reading experience is uninterrupted and unmitigated. Since we literally (and metaphorically) get no breaks, the emotional power of the book, the spectral voices of 45 missing women (from more than 600 young and healthy women reported missing from the city of Juarez, Mexico), gives us no choice but to listen.

Author of three collections, most recently, *Post Romantic*, (University of Washington Press), Kathleen Flenniken has thought deeply on the subject of sections / no sections as she states so eloquently in this passage, sharing how her thinking has changed over time:

When I was organizing my first poetry manuscript a dozen years ago, I thought of sections as the literary equivalent of symphonic movements. I envisioned each section as tonally distinct. I no longer believe so much in those distinctions in my work. Sections imply a categorical tidiness that denies that life and memory is messy, that subject and tone and attitude and love and hate all echo and ricochet and commune together and cast shadows on each other. Removing sections is removing walls. It also removes the reader's convenient breathing place, and that feels right too. I don't want my reader to rest or pull a drawstring tight on one part before launching into another. Every poem is still in play. I like the way a book without sections seems to be in conversation with an older generation of collections that didn't bother with sections or need them. And eliminating sections acknowledges the way so many readers approach a book of poetry, by opening randomly. But really, it's just like any fashion—I want it to feel new, and books without sections feel fresher to me right now.

Like paint colors and hemlines, poetry books are subject to contemporary trends and fashions. Yet the most important consideration is: *what works for you?*

I. Many Ways to Create: Contemporary Poets on Learning from Experience

In recent years there's been much fuss about the order of Plath's <u>Ariel</u>, Ted Hughes version and Plath's original version. The fact is that <u>Ariel</u> is a powerful book either way, but each version represents a slightly different overall vision. At the time Hughes arranged the manuscript, it had to have been difficult, if not impossible, for him to not have been influenced by the effect of Plath's depression and suicide and that is reflected in the arrangement. Plath's version, ending with the famous "bee poems" reflects more of a life force, and perhaps, a more aesthetic vision. In most volumes, the arrangement of poems can make a kind of "arc" or journey and there is not only a single possibility in the work, but several.

~Beckian Fritz Goldberg

More Than the Sum of its Parts:
On Putting Together a Book

~Linda Pastan

From almost the beginning of my writing life, whenever I finished a poem, I was always sure it was the last poem I would ever write. In the same way, I still think every book I publish will be my last. When I recently handed in my fourteenth manuscript, for example, I thought to name it, *Final Poems* or at least *Penultimate Poems*. When I mentioned these titles to my husband, he just laughed, so I'm calling it *Insomnia* instead. Let's start then with titles. I do think they are important—the portal to what is to come—and they're usually easier for a poet to find than for a novelist. If a book contains fifty or sixty poems, one of those poems can usually be counted on to become a good title poem.

My creative energies have waned with age, though I try to make the best use I can of whatever energy is left. But what I described above, what I think of as "Fear of Writer's Block" rather than "Writer's Block" itself, has little to do with me being in my eighties. Nor has the way I put together a book changed much.

Actually, I never think about "The Book" when I'm writing, only about the poem I happen to be working on at the moment. I don't try to keep writing on related subjects, for instance, or to identify and follow themes that might unify a coming book, though certainly they may exist. Instead, I wait until I have 100 or so individual poems finished (this usually takes four or five years) then, moving furniture about as needed, I spread them out on the study floor and gaze at them: So much paper; so many trees!

The next thing I do is to choose the fifty or sixty best poems, or at least the poems that seem to me at that moment to be the best. The rest I might consider good enough to send to magazines, or else I would have left them in a drawer with so many others. But the threshold for being included in a book is higher. (Of course, in many instances I have been wrong in my choices and have had to rectify them later as when a *Selected Poems* came out.) Then I look at the remaining poems, still on the floor, random flowers all, and try to make a bouquet of them, to find not quite accidental relationships between them that can form the kind of patterns that help organize the book. One could always just arrange the poems chronologically, and often very good poets do that. But I like a book to be more than the mathematical sum of its parts. The arrangement should add another dimension, a certain depth or even mystery—should be a kind of poem itself.

Putting together my first book, *A Perfect Circle of Sun,* was relatively easy: four seasons, four sections. And strangely enough, I had about the same number of poems about leaves turning, flowers blooming, walking on the beach, snow falling. The same kind of surprising thing happened two books later with *The Five Stages of Grief.* The poems miraculously fit into Elizabeth Kubler Ross's five stages themselves: Denial, Anger, Bargaining, Depression, Acceptance. Those who know me well might have expected me to have written more poems about depression, or perhaps bargaining, than about acceptance, but that wasn't the case.

My more recent books, however, haven't been as easy to put together. After a lot of thought and experimenting, I was finally able to fit the poems into coherent sections, but the underlying structures seem more abstract than with my earlier work. Still, I always want a book to be broken into some sort of parts, to give the reader a pause, a rest between groups of poems.

Another thing I seem to spend an inordinate amount of time on is choosing which poems face each other. Ideally, two facing poems will rub together and something new will happen, sparks might even be generated. In *Queen of a Rainy Country*, for instance, "What We Are Capable Of," a poem about Abu Ghraib, and "Landscape Near Dachau," harking back to the Holocaust, were written years apart and yet they make, I think, an interesting even disturbing pair—two parts of a new whole. "Firing the Muse" and "Rereading Frost," both in a way about exhaustion with writing, also seem to relate to each other, though they were not originally meant to. This kind of serendipitous thing happens more often than one might expect, so I work hard on choosing where each poem goes. (A few books ago, when my page proofs arrived, I saw that someone had made one mistake in ordering, and consequently all of the poems were opposite the wrong poem. I nearly fainted. Luckily in the age of the computer, it was simple to press a few buttons and fix the whole thing.)

Perhaps I care too much about how my books look, and I do spend a lot of time searching for the perfect cover art. I don't bother much with the covers of other poets' books, I'm usually too eager to read their poems to even notice them, but I certainly care a lot about mine. And I think I may know why. When I published my first book in 1971, I thought that there would be rolls of thunder, that the world—my world at least—would dramatically change. But I quickly learned that when a book of poems is published not a lot happens—a glass of champagne or two with friends to celebrate, a few scattered reviews if you are lucky. The thunder only comes at the moment of holding the finished book and feeling its small heft in your hand, of looking at its cover as if you are seeing it for the first time.

Besides, I read once that at Hawthorne's funeral, a number of his books were placed on top of his coffin. If such a thing were ever to happen again, shouldn't those books be clothed in their best jackets?

As It Is Written

~Spencer Reece

New York City. Fall, 2014. Time passing. You can hear it pass now in all the leaves of the trees, slightly yellowed and stressed at the edges, thousands of drafts of all the poems the trees wrote, soon to be blown into oblivion, irretrievable. *Let go... Let go...* the season says to me. It is my favorite time. I am staying on 18 West 10th Street, the home of friends, Andrew and John: two men married to each other with a son named George, age five. I greet George for breakfast with my coffee. He is in his school uniform. Curiously, the school he is going off to is the same school where my old friend Durell taught: the failed Harvard graduate and my enigmatic spiritually crippled liberator, the subject of the title poem in my book, *The Road to Emmaus*.

Past and present and future collide at the breakfast table with George and the echo of T.S. Eliot's lines from *Four Quartets* hover at the edge of my slurp of coffee: "Time present and time past/ Are both perhaps present in time future/And time future contained in time past." George going to school, hurtling into his future, to the exact rooms where Durell lived and breathed and taught and tread long ago. No, no. Time is not linear. I feel that now. Ghosts clutter a conversation today the way they never did before. Fall falls out the window. Much has changed. Much keeps changing. Much.

The house from which I write to you is the former home of Emma Lazarus, the American Jewish poet who in 1883 wrote the sonnet "The New Colossus." In 1903, the poem was engraved in bronze on the pedestal of the Statue of Liberty. Perhaps it greeted my mother's Lithuanian immigrant ancestors. There was a great diaspora out of Lithuania for America at the turn of the 20th century. Some Jews denied they were Jews. Some Catholics married them and colluded with the burial of their Jewish identities—huddled, pushing, with their devotional books, their black shoes sparkling with sea brine, marrying on the boats, determined to learn English. Such was the story of my mother's people. Lazarus' one famous poem closes:

...give me your tired, your poor,
Your huddled masses yearning to breathe free,
The wretched refuse of your teeming shore.
Send these, the homeless, tempest-tost to me,
I lift my lamp beside the golden door!

I am on the top floor, in a guest room, looking out at the red bricks of the four-story buildings across the street. The sun has turned them a distinct auburn color that belongs to fall, and the cold waves of the Hudson slam like doors on the embankments, and the poor are begging at the corners. Some grape leaves on a balcony have turned papery, as thin as the old newspapers I would find in my Lithuanian grandmother's attic, announcing wars and stock prices and marriages. The present fades into the past and becomes my future. I sit here, writing to you, in gratitude for the lamp of the Statue of Liberty illuminating this little essay and the golden doors of New York that have opened for me, that opened for my relatives, that opened for Durell, that open now for George.

I have perspective these days; I live in Europe now. In Madrid. I serve as the canon to the ordinary for the Bishop of Spain for the Episcopal Church, a fragile branch of the Anglican Communion, as you might imagine, in a country where Catholicism rules. I would have loved to let my Lithuanian Catholic grandmother know that. She was really the only one I ever saw lead a religious life. What compelled me about her religious life is that she never once spoke about it. I was attracted to her lack of promotion. A family trait. One I carry by instinct.

Some years ago. I lived in the only all-girl orphanage in Honduras, a country with 250,000 orphans. There, I worked on an anthology of poems by the girls in the home. A documentary film was simultaneously being made about the process. That book contains my narration that accompanies the girls' poems with film stills. The book will be called *Twelve Love Poems from the Murder Capital of the World*. I hope the book will look like those devotionals that immigrants carried with them as they disembarked on Ellis Island.

Here, in a guest room that probably once housed a maid, an immigrant perhaps, struggling with English I imagine, something I now contend with when speaking my beloved Spanish, which I acquired in middle age, I am waiting for my work visa to come through from the Spanish embassy. Then I will be on a plane and far from New York, the Statue of Liberty, my elderly parents, old friends, this view of ginkgo branches clattering now like empty coat hangers in a closet.

My first book of poems, *The Clerk's Tale*, I worked on for fifteen years, on and off, on and off, while I worked in retail for Brooks Brothers. That book is a talisman of two decades of hopes dashed and dreams reached. The book was rejected nearly 250 times. Then, one surprising afternoon in January of 2003, I returned from work, at the age of forty, to receive a call that the book had won the Bakeless Prize sponsored by Houghton Mifflin. Louise Glück judged. We worked on edits for about six months, between my shifts. I remember distinctly working through the end of the title poem, "The Clerk's Tale," on receipt paper from Brooks, and seeing one of my drafts on a receipt run through the register and into someone's shopping bag.

Louise's voice was a portal to the world of poetry I had dreamed of for many years. Her edits unlocked insights and passages that had stymied me. We ordered the poems in a new way. Because we had never met and the nature of our phone calls was poetically intense, when we *did* meet, after the book had come into the world, we actually had to stand in separate rooms in her Cambridge condominium for the first couple of minutes: it was a shock actually to *see* one another.

I went from standing behind the counter at Brooks to standing behind the podium at the Library of Congress. Unlike three particular heroes I had held close for years—George Herbert, Gerard Manley Hopkins and Emily Dickinson—I was to be published, watched, seen, unmasked. That would require some kind of shift. Not that poets are seen all that much, but still, it is quite different to write entirely for oneself without any hope of publication. The first book had made a particular sound, much of it in isolation. Walking past the White House after the reading was over, I knew I did not want to repeat the sound the first book had made. All the monuments and museums on the Washington Mall seemed to address me and say: *Give it time. Life needs to pass. Experiences need to happen.*

Five more years I stayed on in retail. On vacation breaks, I taught in some low-residency MFA programs for the first time. I waited. Blindly, surprisingly, I found myself volunteering at a hospice and returning to an early desire to follow a religious vocation. I had nearly forgotten that I had once made a run at being a priest in my twenties but I was hopelessly, haplessly immature and ill-prepared. This time, older, I found I had a tremulous and deepening faith carved by life experiences.

Eventually, I retired from Brooks. I left on a Friday and drove up North Berkeley Divinity School at Yale by Monday. I had won a full scholarship to attend three years of seminary. The first question a student asked was: "Sir, what class will you be teaching?" I had forgotten I'd aged.

The second book brewed. Much of the process of making a book, for me, has been unconscious, like a priestly call. A word, a rhyme, a scene, something my mother said, suddenly starts repeating in my head and I cannot shake it.

The second book began to form itself over the next eleven

years—from Florida to New Haven to Europe. Again and again, I began writing down rhythms and sounds. The three years in seminary went into the funnel—the Old and New Testament and Anglican theology and pastoral care and social justice. I handed it in a few years before publication to Jonathan Galassi at Farrar, Straus and Giroux when I was at an artists' colony in Ucross, Wyoming. He was ready to publish, but I said, "No, I need more time." "How long?" he queried. "I don't know," I said, "Maybe five years." In that intervening time, I would send Jonathan updated versions of a manuscript and a few days later with an e-mail, "Not done yet."

Finally, in Madrid, after Honduras, I sent the manuscript to him and said, "Done." He said, "Yes, I think this time you are done, I feel it." Jonathan went over the book carefully and offered editorial suggestions. I took them all.

People say I am an open writer. In my priestly life, I'd translate that as open to the Holy Spirit, and the spirit comes through people and their suggestions; a poem begins, for me, as a porous thing. "Let me read you this," I will start to say to friends who I know can withstand a poetry reading. But there also does come a moment when all the windows and doors of the poem begin to close. I know some poets go back to early work, rewrite, fix, tinker. And there is the famous story of Degas being restricted at the museum entrance with his paint set eager to touch up his ballerina canvases. In my case, I scarcely ever open the book once the author copies arrive, unless I am being asked to sign a book. Prior to the book of poems being mounted for their gallery showing, my studio of poetry is a madhouse of squeezed-out paint tubes and unfinished canvases. But when I am done, finally, I am done. I never go back to the museum with my paint brushes.

The concerns of *Emmaus* were utterly different from *The Clerk's Tale*; something I can only say now that both are done and sitting on a library shelf somewhere. I knew I wanted to try prose poems as I began *Emmaus*. I had never done one before. That challenge led to others. I wanted to try to write a metrical Shakespearean sonnet at the other extreme. I sought out metrical experts to help me. It was almost like signing up for classes in the Charleston and the Fox Trot. I then began to think I wanted the book to be a conversation between these two opposite poles. What happens, I wondered, if you push poetry to prose until it nearly breaks? This pushed some of the longer free verse to verge on language that was very prosy, rather than tight and knowing and rhyme-driven. At one point, in the title poem, I deliberately went through it and took out as much rhyme and metaphor and simile as I could find. It would become a poem that had to shed its art. "Monaco," another of the four longer poems in the book, reads like a fable or short story, but somehow it isn't, it is a poem. Why? And how?

The poems challenged me: all of them nearly, especially the four longer ones, as if the book had these four compass points: "Monaco," "The Road to Emmaus," "Gilgamesh" and "Hartford". "Gilgamesh" was a modern rendering of the Babylonian myth, teasing out the homo-erotic story. "Hartford" was a set of Hildegard von Bingham-like visions, in prose poems, that took on the failed city of Hartford as its subject, along with the immigrant half Jewish, half Christian history of my mother. A fable, a Babylonian myth, a Christian story from the Gospel of Luke and a set of visions—all of the four destinations mysterious and unsolvable. The poems began to teach me things; each one of those long poems set out with a concern or problem and I was somehow naively hopeful I could solve it. But the poems kept telling me they did not want to be solved: "Monaco" (the oldest poem in the book left over from the first book, sixteen or seventeen years old) was about ambiguous sexualities and the more I tried to label the characters in the poem the more they resisted me. "Emmaus" itself was about a closeted gay man whom I had known but who remained ultimately mysterious to me, and why he chose to help me so in my life I never could seem to fully answer. "Gilgamesh" catalogued a big gay love story that ended: why did it end? "Hartford" could never seem to explain my mother or the city. Yet there they were, those poems, laid out to greet me wherever I moved around the world with their questions and very few answers. *Life is mysterious*, the poems kept whispering.

No. I don't fully understand what I did in the first book. Or the second. The themes of the second, I am sure, can find their beginnings in the first. "The Clerk's Tale," by Chaucer, which the title poem references, after all, is about tales told on pilgrimage.

The pilgrimage, for me, got more specific. Damage and anger, necessary pistons in the first book, interested me less. I left much drama at the curb. As I began to notice this shift, I was at first daunted. "What if I have nothing to say if I drop a victim stance?" The ego doesn't like to die. What would drive the book? Reconciliation and forgiveness. Reconciliation and forgiveness were the gasoline and oil that kept the engine running—themes played out in my forties and fifties with my family and in all aspects of my life: spiritual direction, therapy, fourth step inventories from twelve step groups, priestly formation and ordination and beginning work as a priest all began to inform the new direction of the book.

What next? Where does the road go now? Maybe one more book of poems. Perhaps. About my life *in* the church. And, God willing, a decent book of essays. I seek to expound on my gratitude for the poems of Herbert, Hopkins, Dickinson and Merrill to name a few. But who knows? For the moment my prose essays feel like pale assistants to the assistant stage manager, dressed in black with innumerable fanny-packs and head-sets, for a stage mounting of my poems.

The embassy will soon process the visa. My Spanish improves. I just conducted the entire visa interview, standing before a plate glass window, talking to an embassy official with a line of impatient Spanish speakers behind me. Afterwards I walked down Lexington Avenue somewhat stunned. *Did I just do that?* I thought to myself. This giddy flood of new language into my fifty-year-old skull beckons me towards more translations. In *Emmaus* I translated a poem by the Honduran poet, Roberto Sosa. I would like to do more translations, particularly Antonio Machado. His understated Spanish demeanor that created those title-less and short-lined poems fascinate me. The current translations of his work do not always satisfy me.

I work slowly. Be it poetry. Or prose. In the intervening years I completed a narration to accompany the twelve love poems by the girls in the orphanage in Honduras. My prose catalogues the tale of how I turned to priesthood and how the girls in that orphanage affirmed me. Prose humbled me. I rewrote and rewrote. I had a history of journalism, reviewing books, plays and movies for newspapers during my years in retail. Since *The Clerk's Tale*, I have published a few essays. Still a sustained prose effort stood before me as a challenge. For over ten years I have been trying to write something worthwhile in prose. I worked on several versions and struck out in several directions. Many false starts.

But recently, I turned to something spare to accompany the poems of the girls I taught; not memoir, not literary analysis, a quieter thing than that, something from a confessional booth perhaps. A confession. Or a form of praying. George Herbert had written in his poem, "Prayer," that praying was "a kind of tune." The prose I was working on felt like that kind of tune. I don't know exactly what to call it: the girls' poems work contrapuntally against my prose; it feels the most authentic thing for me in prose to explain my priesthood. A memoir felt too centered on me, regarding the call to a profession driven by listening. Hard to pin this newest prose book/anthology down. *The Clerk's Tale*, *The Road to Emmaus* and *Twelve Love Poems* – all three, all mysteries, all remain somewhat inexplicable to me. Just as well, I suppose. When what I write surprises me, in poems or in prose, I feel the Holy Spirit move across the page and screen: that is all I want. I pray for it.

The Ordinary in the Extraordinary:
The Second Collection

~January Gill O'Neil

The hardest thing I've ever had to do as the author of a first poetry collection is publish a second collection. *Underlife,* book No. 1, established me in the poetry community in the way a first book does. I gave readings, guest lectured at colleges, and even read my poems at poetry festivals. With that comes a sense of freedom in being the new poet on the block. No one expects anything from a fledgling poet but a good reading.

With the publication of *Misery Islands,* however, I wrote poems knowing that a few more people were going to read this book. It was a feeling I couldn't shake during the process. And with a title like *Misery Islands*, I imagined the inevitable, somewhat easy, criticism that goes with such a title, from "What a miserable collection!" to "The aptly named *Misery Islands* . . ."

Of course, those fears are all in my head, none of which has happened. None of those fears kept me from writing the best poems of my life. And none of these fears distract me from staying open and finding joy in the everyday world.

The Genesis of Misery

A few summers ago, I was at a local park with my friend, poet Colleen Michaels, who told me the story of Misery Islands. The park is situated off the coast of Beverly, MA, and as she told me the story of the two islands, Great Misery and Little Misery and the captain who was stuck on the island for three days (the captain was miserable; hence, the name), something clicked. I was writing poems about the end of my marriage and wanted something more to pull the poems together. Somehow it all clicked. The poem, "Misery Islands," is also my first real attempt at a long poem. The islands gave me the opportunity to tell many stories at once.

I had been writing quite a while before *Underlife* was published in 2009. My then-husband and I were having problems in our marriage, and poetry became my umbrella. And I needed it. So, I wrote and wrote and wrote. What I didn't want was *Misery* to be therapy, however. And I didn't want the reader's experience to seem as if he or she were peeking in on a nasty fight. The book is so much more than that. It's important to me that the craft comes through.

As with my first poetry collection, I wanted sections. I thought the book would be stronger if I imposed an order. But I miss the days when publishers were less concerned with narrative arcs and themes. Why can't a collection of poems be a collection of poems? Sections are like rest stops for readers. It also allows a dramatic shift in theme and tone. It is nearly impossible to sell poetry in this day and age without a theme or sections to help tell the story. *Misery* needed rest stops to guide the reader through transformation and acceptance.

The Nitty Gritty of Misery

I love the nitty gritty of the publishing industry. So, it pains me to say that I wish I had been more involved with the publication process this time around. I consider myself a hands-on person, one fairly savvy in book production, marketing, and social media. But with so many demands on my free time, I wasn't as involved with the down-and-dirty aspects. Also, my publisher's core production team, who helped birth the first book, had changed significantly and there were points where our visions for the book were not in line. It was less of a collaborative effort, so I stepped back from the process, which was a shame because, like pregnancy, watching something that I produced grow and thrive is really my favorite part of the process.

The photo on the cover is special to me because I kayaked 12 miles roundtrip with a group of friends to Great Misery to take the photo! At one time, Great Misery was a resort for vacationers from Boston. There were cottages and houses on the island, but a fire in the 1920s destroyed everything. The structures were never rebuilt leading to today's terrific lichen-covered ruins all over the island. I have some amazing photos from the excursion.

I did not choose the font, but I am pleased with the publisher's selection. I believe in this book, and so does the publisher, which is important when trying to garner any sort of interest to the book-buying public.

The single most useful thing I learned about creating a book of poems is to only put in the poems I love. Do not put in any filler poems. You know what I mean by fillers—poems that bridge from one idea to the next but are not your best work. Once these poems are published, you're stuck with them. These poems are how your audience gets to know you. So while I don't have any filler poems in either of my two books, as I look ahead at the next project, I'm constantly questioning if the new poems are good poems. I don't want something out there that doesn't represent my best self—even if my best self is a work in progress.

How to Promote Misery

In 2009 when *Underlife* was new, the blogosphere was a booming virtual metropolis. There was an active cluster of blogging sites that poets flocked to because they were community based. Through those interactions, I developed a healthy network, yet I never thought of them as a network. These were poets and writers just like me, shouting into the void to see if anyone was listening. A small group of writers, most of whom I've met and have become friends with, were keen on helping out with blog tours, book reviews, and readings in their hometowns.

Today, I can't keep up with all of the various technologies at my disposal. I use Facebook, Twitter, Blogger (I still blog, but not regularly), Goodreads, Instagram, Amazon.com's author network, Poets & Writers online, Library Thing (I think) and LinkedIn. I rely on search engine marketing as much as the next entrepreneur (you know we're all entrepreneurs, right?) to find readers because we never know how audiences discover our work.

How will I promote *Misery Islands*? This time around, I'm only involved with activities and promotion efforts that bring me joy. Otherwise, why bother. I'll give readings, but not as many because travel puts a strain on homelife. I'll write nonfiction articles and the occasional review, which gets my name out to a wider audience. And, of course, I'll submit new poems for publication. But this time around, I want to work closely with libraries. I may give a series of lectures or workshops for free, and libraries have a built-in base. I truly enjoy the one-on-one exchanges, so meeting new people falls under the "joy" category.

Bottom line: I look for the extraordinary in the ordinary. I write whenever I can—at my daughter's Taekwondo class, my son's flag football games, or the occasional department meeting (if I am so inspired). This semester, I'm making a point of writing when my students write. Nikki Finney suggests writing in the early morning, as early as 4 a.m., before the first cup of tea and first morning chore. That's when I'm still in a half-sleep, half-wake state. None of this has anything to do with publishing, but everything to do with joy.

It's Less Like Rocket Science Than Making Soup

Interview with Diane Seuss

DtM: In this ever-growing poetry world, with so many poets publishing books, what makes for an outstanding poetry manuscript?

DS: An outstanding manuscript, for me, is one that has a distinguishable point of view and is true to its point of view. By that I don't necessarily mean thematic cohesiveness, but—for want of a better phrase—a distinctive aesthetic identity. An outstanding manuscript feels to me as if it has taken its identity, its formal underpinnings, its music, and its approach to language, as far as they could go. Maybe too far. Certainly teetering.

I also would hope that each poem is doing its own work in the collection. Ideally, I'd want every poem to feel crucial in its incremental contribution to the whole rather than more of the same. I had an uncle who would say, when a story someone told would go on too long, "got it. got it. got-it-got-it-got-it." I don't want to get it and have to seek out something else, several pages later, to get.

Despite the barrage of manuscripts in the ever-growing poetry world, each writer has been molded in her own idiosyncratic way. We were all potty trained, I imagine, but each of our potty training went awry in its own unique manner. The same uncle who "got it," when he was a child, would sit on the toilet until a red ring was branded into his ass, then proceed, when his mother finally gave up on him, to leave his offering behind the couch. That's how he was shaped by life. If he had been a poet rather than a traveling salesman, his manuscript, if he were true to himself, ought to have been branded with that same red ring. Maybe the poems themselves would be shaped like the oval of a toilet seat. They'd certainly have been marked with his own particular mélange of resentment, rebellion, sneakiness, and the full-on belief that his little turd was a gift to his mommy, even if she didn't appreciate it.

That uncle is gone, as is his mother. I appreciate a manuscript that knows its own dead, even if it doesn't speak of them overtly. The dead are more interesting than the living. They have nothing left to prove. No work woes or money problems or fitness regimens. They're not caught up in proving themselves worthy. And they can fly. I suggest taking manuscript advice from a ghost rather than a muse. A well-haunted manuscript is often outstanding— but maybe that's a quirk rather than a standard.

DtM: What trick or technique have you learned in ordering your poetry book that could help someone put their first poetry book together?

DS: Crafting a manuscript is an uber-version of crafting a poem. Like a poem, a book has a beginning, a middle, and an end, a fact that can lead us to construct a collection like a linear narrative, but I don't recommend it. There is a deeper trajectory that a manuscript can forge, and the difficult part is finding it, a process that is both instinctual and analytical. Some questions I might explore when putting together a new collection: If this were a single, book-length poem, what is its thesis? Yes, this is a horribly reductive question, but useful in getting at the Tootsie Roll core of the manuscript. Does the book's thesis suggest an ordering principle?

DtM: Is there a single poem that could represent the reader's doorway into the manuscript?

DS: This might not be the flashiest poem in the book, and certainly not the most challenging. This opening poem can function in the way a map's legend functions, or a schoolchild's primer. It can signal to the reader the collection's landscape, its politics, its voice, its music, its symbolic terms, its formal proclivities, or a combination thereof. I can't stress enough the importance of your opening gambit. My second collection received multiple rejections and was a finalist for but not the winner of a few prizes. I changed the opening poem to one that was clear, easily discernible, and set the tone for the whole book. Perhaps it's a coincidence, but the manuscript then received the Juniper Prize and two other offers of publication.

Are you bringing stale assumptions to your thinking about the manuscript? For instance, although many books today are sectioned, not all of them are. Is it possible that yours works best with each poem cascading into the next like uninterrupted dominos? Conversely, might sectioning, especially sections that aren't necessarily chronological, provide a compelling texture or fragmented surface to a manuscript that is feeling somehow rote or habitual? Is the manuscript suffering from too much or not enough cohesion? Is there a way in which the book's order can serve as an antidote to a collection that requires more or less unity? Additionally, consider looking at five books of contemporary poetry that you consider wildly successful. What seems to be each book's organizing principle, and what would happen if your own manuscript emulated it?

Finally, is it all starting to feel over-complicated? Are the poems swimming in front of you like hazy mush? Walk away. Realize it's less like rocket science than making soup. There are many approaches to combining the ingredients, but in the end it tastes pretty good if you're hungry enough. Maybe both of Robert Frost's roads diverged in yellow wood ended up at the waterfall—or the sewage treatment plant. When in doubt, get one well-informed editorial opinion. The editor of my third book told me it had too many sections and that its longest poem, which covered ten pages, belonged at the collection's hub. He was right on both fronts. My gut knew something was off, but without him I wouldn't have recognized it.

DtM: If you could give poets one-sentence of advice in creating their poetry manuscript, what would that advice be?

DS: Get off of social media, crowd-source rarely, if at all, buck trends, get your feet in the dirt, and remember where you're from.

Think Like a Reader

Interview with Gloria J. McEwen Burgess

DtM: What trick or technique have you learned in ordering your poetry book that could help someone put their first poetry collection together?

GB: When you're putting your book together, the best view of your poems is a balcony view. From there, you can take a meta view of your work, your precious poems, which required a view that's up close, detailed, & personal. You'll gain a completely different perspective from the balcony, which will allow you to see the arc of the work.

DtM: If you could give a poet a few words of advice in creating their poetry manuscript, what would that advice be?

GB: Take a page from other art forms. Try approaching your manuscript like a choreographer or composer.

Choreographically, each dance step, each gesture, each movement must have a purpose aligned with the larger purpose of the work. Steps, gestures, movements convey the emotion, spirit, story of the dance. So, too, your poems.

The same is true musically. Each musical element must add to the overall arc of the piece: each note, each phrase, each melodic or harmonic expression. In other words, each of your poems must *earn* its way into the manuscript.

As well, I'd advise finding the pulse or song or through line of your manuscript. When you do, this will assist you in deciding what to leave in & what to leave out. Set aside those poems that don't fit for another manuscript or installation or....

When you find an order you like, treat it like a cup of tea or a loaf of sourdough bread. Let it sit. Let it steep or rest. Sleep on it. Then take a second, third, & fourth look.

DtM: When your first book of poetry came into the world, *Journey of the Rose*, how did you feel? Can you describe your journey?

GB: My first book! I experienced excitement, elation, utter joy, & anticipation. I also experienced relief. And astonishment. I'm sure I said something like, "Oh, my word." Pardon the pun! "Oh, my word. I did it! I can't wait to hold this book in my hands."

My journey began as a poet who wanted to be a "serious" poet, meaning I wanted to see my poems in print. Then I went through a period where I didn't care about being in print. I was far more interested in my poems being relevant. For me, that meant seeking alternative approaches to publication. Hence, I sought out performative platforms & collaborations with artists in imaginal media, including moveable & permanent installations. For example, several of my poems were "published" in a non-traditional medium, published as part of a bridge at Brown University, a glass bridge connecting the Arts & Engineering Schools.

Regardless of medium, my excitement & joy & relief was the same.

DtM: Do you have any extra tips?

GB: Think like a reader, a desirous consumer of your poems. But edit like a professional editor.

A Self-Help Guide for Getting Along
with Your Manuscript

~Melissa Studdard

A manuscript is a love and a crush. You wake in the middle of the night thinking about it, delighted, frustrated, alternately and unpredictably elated and insecure. Though you know you need to give it space, you sometimes feel the shameful urge to smother and control it. In some ways, this relationship feels similar to others you've had or heard about, yet it's also wholly unique. Such are the woes and joys and mysteries of love. But as anyone who has seen a good counselor knows, there are universal, practical strategies that can apply to even the most seemingly individualized and fervid situations.

Listen:

First and foremost, listen to what your poems are telling you. It may seem easier to wrangle them into formation, but like any other curious creatures, as soon as you get them lined up, they're going to pop out and have to be coaxed back in. Trust me, it's easier to just start with negotiation and compromise. Ask the poems what they want. You may have created them, but they've taken on their own lives now, and they have both intelligence and personality.

Fan them out and see how they look in conversation with each other. And I really do mean fan them out. At this stage, it's important to bring them from the screen to the physical world where you can bodily move them around. This may look slightly different from one manuscript or person to the next—maybe you'll sit circled by them on the floor; maybe you'll tack them all over a wall and move them around for a week or a month. The critical things are that you start to view them as objects that can be relocated, and that you live with them in your literal space for a time. In the same way that you can sit staring at the computer for hours with no idea what to write and then find yourself flooded with ideas as soon as you start vacuuming, you can also walk past the poems on your way to the bathroom and suddenly see a pattern emerge. The longer you can keep them in your physical space, the more you will see.

Consult:

Talk to your friends and family members, hire editors, buy coffee for random people in cafés while thrusting your manuscript at them; do whatever it takes to get the objective perspectives other people offer. You'll always be too close to your manuscript to do it alone. You need the insights of people not already fantasizing about china patterns (or layout designs) with your book. Their distinct mindsets and life experiences bring a shift in perception that can be likened to having shaken the object chamber of a kaleidoscope. The same colors are still there, but the view is different. They can tell you what is not conveying fully, what you've said too many times in too many ways, what doesn't fit. These are sometimes things you cannot see yourself because the poems are already connected in your mind 1) by the fact that you created them, and 2) by links that fire so strongly in your own synapses that you don't even realize you have not transferred them to the page.

Plan:

The earlier, the better. Spontaneity may seem more romantic, but organization is not antithetical to creativity! Organization can unleash creativity in the same way a constraint, such as writing sonnets that all begin with the word "floccinaucinihilipilification" can help you stumble upon concepts and connections you would have never explored otherwise.

For my first poetry collection, I began the organization process after I'd written most of the poems, in much the same manner I described above—papers spread on the floor for a week until they spoke to me, poems and lists tacked to walls. Then, a friend showed me how to use the *Table of Contents* function in MS Word, and everything changed. It sounds simple, I know, but once I created the table, I began to see patterns in my work and write into them. I realized I was writing not one book, but three, and I created three separate documents, which all have their own tables.

If you don't know how to use this function, I highly recommend watching an online tutorial and getting started right away. Because the table numbers and renumbers the pages for you and makes it easy to create, reorder, and move sections, you can conceptualize the whole book as you go. It's like your lover now has a magical, transparent skull that allows you to understand the structure of their thought process so that you'll hardly have any more misunderstandings at all.

Since I've discovered the TOC function, I've gone from writing poems to writing books of poems. I'm always aware of where a poem fits and how it reflects on the book as a whole, because I can see it all laid out in front of me and morphing as a single organism *while* I am creating it. My days of writing poems before it feels as muddled as a brain on adolescent hormones.

Emulate:

You know that great couple down the street that always seems so in love? Go ahead. Copy their weekly date night or ballroom dance lessons or nightly tea hour. Just as you have role models for the kinds of poems you want to write, find role models for the kinds of books you want to write. There are so many ways to organize a collection—through narrative, motif, a philosophical or emotional trajectory, a question that is pursued and either answered or not, through categorizing human behavior according to the mating rituals of different mammals.

Pay attention to the collections you like. What do they have in common? How do they move? I often like collections that feel helical, spiraled, or braided, with multiple concepts, themes, and images reappearing and gently coiling around each other. My mind craves complex stimuli and fires better when it has multiple things to consider simultaneously. Others prefer poems and collections that are more tightly focused and build and release tension. Take the time to compare the books you admire and find the threads that will help you better know yourself.

Keep It Fresh:

I once interviewed Marge Piercy for a podcast, and she said it's important to vary your work thematically and by tone when giving a literary reading. She said if you read too many love poems in a row, for instance, the audience will start thinking about their own love lives. I feel it's the same with manuscripts. Although we seek, to a certain degree, cohesion, we also do not want to send the reader into a lull or trance. The manuscript needs surprises, turns, lifts, and dips, as well as refrains. Periodically show up unexpectedly to the page with a bottle of wine or a new negligee. Your manuscript, and your readers, will thank you.

Be Flexible:

When it comes to love, you can't afford to be stubborn. When you change one thing, other things change too. Keep re-evaluating and recalibrating as you go. Should a poem be taken out? But it's one of your favorite poems? Take it out anyway and save it for another book. Should more poems be added? But you're tired of writing poems? Add them anyway. Your lover is worth it. You should stay as fluid, open, and generative as possible throughout the process. If you're afraid of losing something, keep a record of the various stages so you can revert back to or include elements from a previous iteration.

Finally, your relationship with your manuscript, like all good relationships, is about trust. Once you've put in the work, you should trust that you and your manuscript know what's best. Don't get cold feet just as you're about to walk down the aisle. Don't fear or second guess your decisions. If you've been paying attention and listening to your manuscript's need, when the time comes, you'll know exactly what to do.

Rebirth, Navigation, Survival

Interview with Lee Herrick

DtM: In this ever-growing poetry world, with so many poets publishing books, what makes for an outstanding poetry manuscript?

LH: An outstanding poetry manuscript, in my mind, operates well on conceptual, emotional, and structural levels simultaneously. In other words, on a conceptual level, it has some compelling, unifying element such as theme, tone, form, or story, even if it is a wide-ranging manuscript. When I have finished reading it, I feel moved or deepened on some emotional scale. My anger, sadness, compassion, doubt, hope, or love has been reshaped, reconsidered, and rendered more whole. I sense an urgency that triggered the poems, some fire or smolder. There is a natural gravity at work. I am surprised. It feels new. As a result, I see the world in a new way, and I see myself in relationship to it in a new way. It is also mindful of craft, which is sometimes a subtle, underlying richness that sets manuscripts apart. This can relate to form, the line, titles, or even a complete, conscious abandonment or rewriting of it. I feel trusted and therefore I trust the poems. I begin to believe in them. This deepens the manuscript, the experience for the reader, and I would imagine, the creative experience for the poet.

DtM: What trick or technique have you learned in ordering your poetry book that could help someone put their first poetry book together?

LH: With *Scar and Flower*, my third book, I was more in tune with the range of emotional notes in the poems and the number of poems about gun violence, trauma, suicide, or other deaths. With order, then, I wanted to begin with a softer, more contemplative warm-up of sorts before the heavier poems about death. I struggled with how many consecutive poems about shootings or other deaths I could string together, nor just for the readers' sake but for my own. I found that I (and in most cases, the reader) could handle more difficulty and heaviness than I thought. So, *Scar and Flower* is in two sections: first, scar, as in a wound, a death, hurt, damage, or violence; and second, flower, as in recovery, rebirth, navigation, survival, coping, or grace. I didn't want to make it completely binary, though, as our lives and the ways we experience trauma are anything but binary, so I infused a small handful of "scar" poems in the second section, and a small handful of "flower" poems in the first section. What I mean to say is that I thought a lot about the emotional resonance of the poems individually, collectively, and what I wanted the book to feel like, on the whole. Looking back at the last poem in my three books, I realize that I like to end on a note of hope, imagination, or if I can, grace.

My first book, *This Many Miles from Desire*, is organized in sections by theme. Some books organize by a story arc or by chronology. I found it helpful in *Scar and Flower* to be open to changing the titles of the poems. I changed about a third of the poem titles in the book in the late stages of revision, something I'd never done. This helped unify the manuscript, I think. Ultimately, reading a wide range of books from the last few years and going back forty or fifty years gives us a context in which to imagine and envision your own book. It allows you to be purposeful and true to yourself, your poems, and ultimately, the book.

DtM: If you could give a poet a few words of advice in creating their poetry manuscript, what would that advice be?

LH: Think about what emotion, experience, story, or idea is driving the manuscript on a fundamental level. In other words, what urgency or need or desire made you write these poems or made these poems come through you? In addition to (or aside from) all the workshops, the craft talks, and the social media noise, remember what fuels you (and the poems that will comprise the manuscript). Is it some insatiable curiosity, a question, an absence, a violence, a death, an experience, an idea? Have you worked through it enough, or is there more it wants from you? Is it unified enough, or are there two or three different manuscripts here?

Theoretically, this means writing the most authentic, unique poems you can. Read as much as you can. Learn what books are around you, so you can know how yours is unique. Revise, re-vision, and be able to let go. Cut the poems that you doubt. Have smart friends who will tell you what's not working and listen to them. Titles are important. Be mindful who you share the manuscript with. Find or return to your trusted people and places. Give it time. Don't rush. You have to believe in your poems.

DtM: Can you describe the mixture of emotions your first book entailed for you? Can you describe your journey?

LH: My first book, *This Many Miles from Desire*, was published in 2007. I wrote it over the course of ten years, often in journals while traveling in Latin American and Asia. It felt surreal to hold it when it was published. I remember how excited I was to read from a book at an event. It felt surreal because after being such a reader of books, I was the author of one. I was doing interviews, flying across the country for invited readings and book signings, and meeting people I'd admired for many years. What surprised me was how many different audiences read my book, as well as how much deeper and richer my experience in the Korean adoption community became. I did a book signing in Seoul, South Korea, the country where I was born. I did events in people's homes for book clubs, small rural libraries, museums, schools, universities, and large conferences. I met people from all walks of life all over the country. It felt like a whirlwind. It deepened my sense of gratitude. Some wonderful friendships began. I learned a lot along the way. Over time I was better able to be in the moment for each interview, for each dinner, for each reading. It felt like a beautiful blur. It's true that the first book is a unique, emotional, unforgettable journey. Mine definitely was, and I'm forever grateful.

Different Kinds of Outstanding

Interview with Maggie Smith

DtM: In this ever-growing poetry world, with so many poets publishing books, what makes for an outstanding poetry manuscript?

MS: I doubt there are two poets who would answer this question the same way. There are so many different aesthetics, different kinds of "outstanding," which is why the poetry world continues to expand. I never know which books will take hold of me and refuse to let go—books as varied as Claire Wahmanholm's *Wilder,* Ada Limón's *The Carrying,* Camille Rankine's *Incorrect Merciful Impulses*, and Darren C. Demaree's *Two Towns Over.* These books are so different but they are wholly, unabashedly themselves. The poems feel true to me—their speakers, their emotional registers, their metaphors. I believe them.

DtM: What trick or technique have you learned in ordering your poetry book that could help someone put their first poetry book together?

MS: I often prefer series spread throughout a manuscript instead of together in a single section. It can be a way to pattern the book and to provide moments of familiarity for readers when they encounter them throughout instead of back-to-back-to-back.

DtM: If you could give a poet one-sentence of advice in creating their poetry manuscript, what would that advice be?

MS: Think of how the poems in your manuscript might be in conversation: which poems spark off of one another, and which transitions would be the most impactful?

The Mighty Meta: The Language of Your Book
   (As a Book)

~Sandra Beasley

The first time I encountered "meta" in a literary context was in a beloved graduate seminar on metafiction. *Meta*, I learned, came from the Greek term for "beyond," and indicates an enriching gesture that references the work's own conventions. In the familiar language of cinema, a character breaks the fourth wall by looking at the camera. In the texts of authors such as Italo Calvino and Julio Cortázar, it's a moment that reminds us that what we're reading is a made literary artifact.

Not everyone values thinking of one's poetry book *as a book*. There is historical context for this; some of our greatest contributions to literature are bound sheaves of pages gathered into de facto "books" by family or executors. But let's temporarily privilege the opportunity to dialogue with an editor about the shape of one's work in the world. Let's admit the times that you've dreamed of your cover design. You're doing the work to engage a press by finding the opportunities, writing the cover letters, and (all too often) paying the reading fees.

You cannot be your book's best advocate until you understand what your text is trying to do. To clarify, what your book is doing is not the same as what *you* were doing in the period of time that you wrote this book. The book cannot be a vestigial remnant of your creative energy. Don't litter the collection with inside references and indulgences. Your book has the power to be a self-contained catalyst that sparks revelation in the reader. Until you find that version, it won't rise to the top of the slush pile.

What is your meta-text? Consider:

- The manuscript title

- Table of contents (accumulated poem titles)
- Epigraphs
- A preface poem or "proem"
- Section breaks (which may or may not introduce additional titles)
- Any epilogue, in prose or poem form
- Endnotes

A title can be pithy or provocative, enigmatic or humorous, prioritizing a first-person speaker or advocating a worldview. There's no singular approach. But there is this practical fact: if your manuscript's title exceeds four words in length, casual correspondence will adopt a one- or two- or three-word shorthand for your title. Make sure it's a phrase you feel good about—and challenge yourself to be sure that it's not the phrase (as a pointer to a larger idea) that you should choose instead.

Poem titles can and should vary, but parallel structure in titling is an effective way to encourage your reader to put poems "in conversation" that aren't immediately adjacent on the page. For teachers, a table of contents that announces such dialogues is a goldmine for working with students learning to find patterns. A table of contents can sustain three or even four such series, or can hunker down and promote one in particular.

Think of your epigraph(s) as an opportunity to indicate investment in a secondary genre—music, cinema, visual arts—or as a way to emphasize an underlying context, such as faith or history. Or simply put a phrase that evokes delight! This is an art, not a science. But if you cite an author, be aware that you're forging an implicit bridge to that author's work, and the reader who crosses that bridge will probably compare the two.

Preface poems, section breaks, and epilogues will all tempt the poet who is drawn to thinking about rhythm and syncopation in text. Each pause is an opportunity for inflection. These are also the moment where the stagecraft of the manuscript is most evident. Do chorus figures wait in the wings, with a need to step forward and comment on the larger presentation? What is being labeled? Is there a jump in time and tense? Does the poet crave direct dialogue with the reader, a sense of being "heard" that might relate to the collection's larger confessional instinct?

These instincts can easily inform the endnotes, as well. The more invested the poet is in terms of being credited with research and documentarian instincts, the longer the endnotes tend to be. Endnotes might also emphasize artistic inspirations in order to situate the book in the landscape of a "school" or cultural moment.

When we share manuscripts with trusted friends, our questions tend to focus on ordering and possible cuts; in other words, we are still fixated on the value of the individual poem. Try asking your reader for a reaction to the book's meta-text. Send them your table of contents (TOC)—and *only* your table of contents—and request the following, with the assurance that you know this is guess-work:

- Three words that might evoke the collection's thematic concerns
- Three adjectives (or a short phrase) to describe the collection's tone
- A suggested *type* of epigraph; not the words, per se, but a style of source
- Two titles from your TOC that could double as attractive titles for the book

One of the pragmatic advantages of doing this is that it is an easy ask, an hour's work for your friend versus a day's labor. More importantly, this feedback is designed to get you thinking about the forest rather than the trees. If the response you get matches your own conception of the book, look for presses that publish books kindred to this manuscript. But if the response diverges, don't dismiss it as the reader's failure. Either change the book's meta-text to better reflect the poems, or be honest with yourself about the conversation this book wants to have with the world.

All Things are Born to Change Their Shapes: The Story of Organizing a Poetry Chapbook

~Jennifer Martelli

I. Anxiety

The thought of organizing my own poetry manuscript gives me anxiety. Right now, as I write this, I can feel my diaphragm tighten just thinking of how a pile of poems should be "speaking to each other," when I can't hear what they're saying!

It's as if I walked into a room of friends and they all suddenly clam up or I find myself in the middle of a conversation where I'm lost and just keep nodding my head, "yes, yes." I should know these poems—I wrote them! I *can* write and revise a poem; I have no fear of rejection. I've published three books of poetry, all with a chapbook that came before—like a stone within a fruit. I'm drawn to the chapbook for its intensity and its concentration, its brevity. I love the rustic look of a chap; the way its spine is stapled or stitched. I can see the bones. My previous chapbooks were easy to organize; they were all chronological, with very specific, historical topics.

When I expanded these chaps into full-length books, I brought my tangled messes to friends. Usually, I was close to tears. Why won't my poems speak to each other? Having smart, kind, honest, and brutal friends is useful, but I wanted a method—tools—to get me to that place of organizing that feels internal, organic. I also wanted to do this without the drama of a panic attack. I understood the *concept* of organizing a manuscript, but I didn't have a deep feeling for it, beyond angst. I needed help!

II. Birthday Party Love!

In February, 2021, I gave myself a birthday gift of a class on manuscript organization called, *From Manuscript into Book: Demystifying the Process* offered by Poets on the Coast. I had a pile of about 30 poems, not quite enough for a full-length book. These pieces acted like they belonged together (maybe I could hear them whisper each to each). They weren't part of a project per se, that is, there was no one defining topic (as opposed to my previous books that focused on Kitty Genovese and Geraldine Ferraro). With these poems, I felt like a terrible party host, or a mother at a forced play date. How would I get these poems to speak up more? Could they create their own community?

III. The Tools and The Map

I adore school supplies, so right away I was smitten by the first two suggestions that the facilitators, Susan Rich and Kelli Russell Agodon, offered us:

> 1. **Invest in a spring binder**: These are gorgeous, yet pricey binders that hold papers together by springs, as opposed to holes. Traditionally, they were always a serious black faux leather. Now, they come in a broad rainbow of colors and are available from several online shops. You can reuse them after your book has been accepted, which it will be. This binder will become the home for your book—and only for your book. You can pull pages out, put new poems in, move them around without having to cut or poke anything! Every time you create changes and additions, the spring binder lets you begin your manuscript anew.

> 2. **Buy a journal or notebook to dedicate to the process**: I use Moleskine mini notebooks because of their convenient size. I kept mine right in my binder. This is for any notes about the book—and only the book. I write any organizational ideas in this notebook. Example: *I should switch those two poems; I should change the*

title; move one section to the beginning. Do I dare get excited about this manuscript? Do I join the worldwide poetry party?

It is vital to me that these tools have one purpose: to help me wrangle this manuscript into order. These tools are tactile. I could decorate them if I wanted, but I loved the austerity of a black binder and a gray journal. Maybe that says something about me?

I had my tools, now I needed my map. I was given two brilliant suggestions by poets January Gill O'Neil and Diane Seuss:

1. Think of the book in three sections; perhaps

    a. an outer scaffolding
    b. an interior world/conflict
    c. an emergence to the world/resolution

I'm a superstitious ex-Catholic. Three is sturdy, balanced. It's my lucky number.

2. Start the book simply: choose a poem that isn't overly complex or too long, but more so, that introduces the reader to their experience in reading the book. I had an idea to create my three sections. I chose the first poem, "How to Make a Moat," for two reasons: first, the "how to" title implies direction; second, it's a short prose poem, and I liked the neatness of the form.

I had seen a call from Small Harbor Editions for a hybrid chapbook contest with a longer page-limit. The poems I brought seemed perfect; the chapbook-length also seemed less daunting. I went out and bought my binder (I bought three), printed out the poems, and moved them into their temporary home. For the first time, I felt excited about trying out these new tools.

I could intuit some obvious groupings: witch poems; poems

based on Sylvia Plath; poems rooted in Greek and Christian mythology. These would all work as sections, but it felt very superficial, very "meh." Very ordinary. Keeping the "rule of three" in mind, I thought of an old working title a friend had suggested. It was taken from a line in one of the poems, "The thigh. The clavicle. The moon. . . ." This felt right to me; this series of images was not made up of abstract nouns but actual things, with surfaces and textures and depth. That this series also was embedded in a three-part poem in the book; this made it feel less arbitrary to me. My intuition clicked with my tools and I began sorting.

IV. My Three Teams

> 1. **Team Thigh**: A lot of the poems in the book concerned themselves with women transformed into other objects, like trees or smoke or blood, so any poem that either mentioned a body part or had a soft "fleshiness," went into this pile.

> 2. **Team Clavicle**: I am a sucker for bones and skulls— and there are a lot in this collection. I was interested in the contrast between the softness of the flesh and the underlying structure. I also love the sound of "clavicle." Any poem with a bone, skeleton, or skull was put on this team.

> 3. **Team Moon**: One of my many phobias is suffocation; as I wrote in a poem that was written in response to Plath's "Berck-Plage," *I am obsessed with women suffocated.* The Team Moon poems contained images of the moon, rock, cement—anything that wasn't human.

I liked this organization because I felt that the structure was embedded in a poem deep in the book. Now, I could see—and hear—this collection better. I felt I had a way to cull poems that might not belong or to see where I needed to write a new poem.

Keeping in mind the lead poem, "How to Make a Moat," I switched Team Thigh with Team Clavicle because I wanted to start with a shorter poem that established the themes in the book:

> *If I were to make a moat, I'd use the shoulder blades of a larger mammal to dig up sedges that bend the way corn stalks bend to form hieroglyphs seen from the sky. I could do it in a night, too, but I'd have to wait for a storm to fill my moat with rainwater.*

I also felt that the three sections, in this order, conveyed a sense of movement: inner (bone/clavicle)-outer (thigh)-beyond (moon). I was able to look at each section as a mini-chapbook as well. I aimed to keep the sections fairly equal in their poem/page count because I wanted stability. In my final organization, I took out physical section breaks not only to accommodate the page count, but I didn't feel this book needed the space, the breathing room. I liked the smooth movement of the chap beginning with a bony prose poem and ending with a bloody moon prose poem. My panic had been quelled by a spring binder and a little notebook!

V. Success!

Without my usual angst (which in itself can be anxiety-provoking; I am suspect of my own confidence), I thought these poems were finally talking. I could hear something; I actually understood the conversation, even if just a little bit! I wasn't completely sure if I felt that the book was "done," or that I simply had a sense of relief that I was beginning to understand something about organization or structure. I sent my chapbook out into the world with what I felt was a backbone, a spine—and not the stapled, sewn kind. The "rule of three" provided the internal structure I couldn't achieve before; it felt right—organic and literary at the same time. I submitted to the Small Harbor Editions Hybrid Chapbook Contest in March, 2021. And wow! I was notified that July that my chap, *All Things Were Born to Change Their Shapes*, had won! I still have the email archived! The title, which is a line from Ovid's *Metamorphoses*, felt so right as well! My book had changed its shape. Its inner workings—which were evident only to me— seemed to integrate the collection.

I am grateful for the tools and the map I was given in the Poets on the Coast workshop. I'm using this method now to organize a full-length manuscript. It's allowed me to move my poems in a way that feels far more organic, yet intentional. It's given me a way to enter my poems with a clearer eye and ear; a way to organize and cut; to see what's missing. I've used these tools to help friends organize their manuscripts. As co-poetry editor of *The Mom Egg Review*, one of my duties is to arrange the poetry for each print issue. We usually publish 50-60 poems; I've used January's and Diane's tools to help structure the poetry section—which is about the length of a manuscript, but with each poem speaking in its own voice!

I had an old friend who would tell me that I needed to take an "objective view" of my own life. I think this applies to my poetry. I think I needed a way into my own work; a way to enter the flesh and bones of my own poetry. I'll probably always have some anxiety around organizing my own manuscript. Yet, with my sober binders and little notebooks, I now have the wherewithal to navigate and to enter these baffling cocktail hour conversations that my poems have with each other.

Righting the Manuscript: Seven Techniques

~Lauren Camp

Your remarkable manuscript...you've worked so hard on it and believe in what you've created. And you should. But what if it isn't getting the attention it deserves yet? A manuscript does the best first for the writer, who had something to address and explore, and then for the readers who engage with the finished product.

I've been lucky. Twice I've been told by book editors, "This manuscript was nearly perfect. There was almost nothing to be done to it." This is a good goal. This is my always goal.

How do you get there? By troubling the words, the line, the syntax, your subject and the arrangement every which way. Poetry is a sublime art form, but making it takes time. Breathtaking poems generally emerge from a slow, considered approach and a long gestation period.

Your book needs to be published, so let's see what we can do. Here are seven hands-on techniques to help move your poems toward becoming a book.

All the Revision You Can Do

Students have asked me, "Where do my less effective poems belong in the manuscript?" Instead of burying them in the middle, take them out, or preferably, make those poems equal in quality to the others. It's nice when you're doing readings from the finished book and find you can open to any poem and what you land on will be worth reading aloud to an audience.

Maybe this is the most obvious step, the careful attention to each poem. Ruthlessly, read the work aloud. (I read to my deaf cat who sits and purrs no matter what.)

Have you gone on patrol for all the adverbs? Leave some, sure, but consider every instance they appear. Can you better muscle the verbs? Ask them to lift the line. Also, claim only the "ing" words you need. That form, a present participle from a verb, is so kind. The word will whisper over readers. Be sure you need to be "going" when it is more direct to "go"—or better yet, "fly," "meander," or "trudge."

In each poem, desire the details. Novelist Lorraine Hansberry talked about "the universality of specificity." This is a phrase I share often with my students. The reader needs those details to "see" what you're saying.

Order, Disorder or Betwixt

You have choices in organizing. You can cluster poems together around a theme or sprinkle the topics around. Does your manuscript need straight focus: one poem after the next? Does it split neatly into sections? If you divide into groupings, try to limit how many you have. I'm partial to three, an odd number. Try for a similar number of pages in each section.

But rules are meant to be broken sometimes. *One Hundred Hungers* told such an indirect story, encompassing poems about Baghdad in the 1940s with others set in 1970s America. I had many holes in the story I was trying to tell and needed to pull the parts together in some logical way. I ended up with five sections in which the reader reenters the story at different places and is given new information or perspective. I put both time periods into each section. In a way, each section became an everything, a stand-alone story. And the whole became five times everything.

Have you tried reordering? For months, I thought I knew precisely which poem would be first in *One Hundred Hungers*. As it turned out, that poem landed on page 62 in the finished book. I had found a better way to enter, one that surprised me as much as I hoped it would engage the reader. When I moved that once-first poem toward the back of the book, other elements needed to shift as well. Revision is about exploring new options, but that's hard to do when you're determined to stay true to your initial intent. Loosen up.

Stroll or Fight

Some poems have tremendous energy and forward motion; others are quieter. I like a poem that kicks me in the gut, but I can't read a whole book of gut-busting poems. I need variety. I need some breaks in the action (or inaction). Let the reader ease in sometimes, and other times make them see and feel the hard stuff.

I arrange the pages on a large table, lining up the poems in the order I want them. I walk around slowly, scratching my head, reading for threads and connectors. It's easy to slip other poems in front or behind. I venture everything. I spend those ordering days asking *what if, what if* .... When, hours later, my feet and back are tired, but I think I have a good read, I put the poems, in my selected order, in a binder and stash the whole thing out of sight for a month or more.

Until I nearly forget it. That's how I keep rebuilding "fresh eyes."

Recently, I read through a manuscript that I'd put together many months before. I hadn't looked at it in all that time. About four-fifths of the way through, I felt "this would be a good ending to the book." There were still many poems to go. I turned the page and continued reading. Two poems later, I had the same thought. Instead of trying to make all those extra poems work, I cut them. Thirteen poems leaner, the manuscript seems much stronger. Ironically, the quick answer to finding what works is never quick.

Down to the Notes

I did a talk about my fourth book, *Turquoise Door*, at the Georgia

O'Keeffe Museum one autumn. After the talk, one of the gentlemen who had been in the audience came up with his copy for me to sign. He asked who had assembled the notes at the back of my book. He was so grateful for the information gathered there. This was my most dreaded part of the manuscript to assemble, but I'm glad I went to the effort. It gave me a place to collect historical facts and other details that didn't belong within the poems.

Some readers turn to this section of a book first. Don't overlook this chance to explain or better define the poems if it will help your reader. Maybe even consider a bibliography if your book warrants it.

Gather Credit Lines

Get the work into journals. Do the grueling and ego-daunting work of submitting. Two submissions a month, perhaps. If you're motivated, do more. Pick the best time to plant yourself in a chair and get the work organized and out there. I try to do submissions at the start of the month. Someone else I know does one submission each week. You will absolutely gather disappointments. Every normal person does. So what? Keep going.

Think of this as a chance to connect your poetry to the right audience. To gift your words and perspective to those who may not realize they need it.

Alongside this lovely gesture, you are also building an acknowledgments page for the back of your book. Some presses like to know that journal editors have chosen the work they're considering. Furthermore, editors who have selected your work for their journal will be inclined to cheer about the book "their" poem is in. Journal readers who connect with the work also begin to care about and follow your writing.

Factoring Some Other Possibilities

How about changing the speed? Are you building an arc? What if that comes early instead of in the typical middle place?

A former poet laureate and I were talking about judging contests one day. Three poems into the manuscript, if the work hasn't entranced, the poet moves on to the next contest entry. So, if that's all the chance you get to sway a judge, think hard about where your manuscript starts.

Also, don't submit absolutely everywhere. Consider the press you want to be with and also notice who the contest judge is. Does that judge's aesthetics align with yours?

Look carefully at the poems that bookend the collection. Do you want to begin with a *proem* (a prologue poem that starts the book)? With such a prominent place, that poem needs to have strength and intrigue. The last poem is critical, too. What should go in that prime space? A poem that clicks the manuscript neatly closed, or one that opens new possibilities, that lets the reader look out at the distance the poems have offered? Think hard about this prime spot.

Repeat to Repeat

I watch for repeats in two ways: the words and the poems.

One of my last steps on a manuscript draft is to gather every word of it and dump the whole thing into an online program (I'm partial to *Wordcounter*) that tells me how many times I've used the same word. This means, in truth, that I am not at the end of revision, but have a way and a reason to go back in and tighten. Who needs the word "moon" 82 times, after all?

I also think it's worth considering whether you've said this same thing slightly more magnificently in another poem. I write the same subjects over and over. I know not all of those poems will make it into a manuscript.

Finally, never feel you have to copy anyone else. Each poem you are looking for is inside you. The material is yours, and it is good enough. You just have to challenge yourself to climb into your truest, most unboundaried voice, and to give your reader a way to navigate through.

Try to Enjoy the Process

Interview with Jose Hernandez Diaz

DtM: In this ever-growing poetry world, with so many poets publishing books, what makes for an outstanding poetry manuscript?

JHD: I think the voice has to pull the reader in immediately. Yes, many books are being published right now. It is so easy to move on to another book if the book you're reading doesn't wow you. It can be an intellectual wow, emotional, visceral, aesthetic wow, various wows, but it has to captivate you completely.

Other qualities that make a great manuscript: balance, subtlety, hyperbole, persona (done right), great imagery, sound, rhythm, political vigor, humor, wit.

DtM: What trick or technique have you learned in ordering your poetry book that could help someone put their first poetry book together?

JHD: Since I tend to write either poetry in verse or prose poetry, I usually split the poems up by themes or narrative perspective. For example, the first section of my full-length manuscript is family-based themes & first-person poems in verse; then political themes & first-person verse poetry; then first-person prose poems; then third-person prose poems; etc.

DtM: If you could give a poet a few words of advice in creating their poetry manuscript, what would that advice be?

JHD: Patience is the hardest and most important aspect to the poetry manuscript process. At first, it will feel ready and you will submit it everywhere. Maybe it will land or maybe it will get rejected. If you make a finalist list, that's a good sign. Keep trying to improve it. If you start making some pretty big, prestigious finalist lists, the manuscript might not need much work and you might want to keep submitting it as is. Patience is hard, yes, however, now I can see that I'm glad my manuscript wasn't picked up early or prematurely, because it needed a couple years to figure itself out.

DtM: Your first book is about to come into the world! Can you describe the mixture of emotions this book entails for you? Can you describe your journey?

JHD: Excitement, of course, and also, nerves. How will it be received? How will it feel when someone on *Goodreads* writes the first bad review? What will the cover of the book look and feel like? Then, of course, in a pandemic year, those of us who've had our book tours canceled can remember an even greater disappointment.

Try to enjoy the process of promotion, readings, etc. You only have one first time. Take a moment to understand what you've accomplished. Nothing was inevitable. You've worked for this. Stayed up editing. Went through rejection after rejection. Disappointment after disappointment. Wanted to give up. Now you have your own book! Congratulations.

In Working Order, or Proxemics
and the Poetry Book

~Anna Leahy

In an article by culture writer Allyssia Alleyne titled "This Is Your Brain on Tidiness: The Psychology of 'Organization Porn'," photographer and Instagrammer Emily Blincoe says, "You could take a photo of a bouquet of flowers or you could spend five hours clipping the tops and arranging them by gradient." And as goofy as that may sound, that distinction in flower-arranging, it seems to me, has everything to do with how poetry books are organized. Which books are vases bursting with lush blooms, and which books are "hyper-organized" arrangements? What's the range in between, and why does this matter—or seem to matter? Blincoe offers one way of thinking that's akin to a poet's: "It's just another way of looking at things that other people aren't willing to put in the time for." A way of looking that other people don't take time to do might be considered expertise. I enjoy looking at flowers or tasting wine, appreciate the experience, and even feel such experiences enrich my life, but I don't have expertise in the realms of flowers or wine.

Alleyne's article goes on to suggest, "Though the individual components depicted are familiar, the new content requires that the viewer look for more than just literal meaning in the image." Poets too are going for more than literal meanings. Then, Alleyne points to experimental psychologist Johan Wagemans, who goes further: "Usually, perception is after meaning, but when you start playing with images in a way like this, it's clear that it's not about meaning, it's about the special relationship between things and how they form a group or a composition." Now, we're really onto something for poetry. While individual poems have meaning, a book is a composition formed by a large group of poems. Tidiness isn't where we're going with poetry, but the very materiality of a book—even in a digital format—is not a haphazard mess either.

Maybe a rose is a rose is a rose, but a rose among roses or among tulips and orchids is both a rose and part of a bouquet or garden. I'm interested in principles that underpin a poetry collection's organization and thereby orchestrate the experience of the book as a book as well as the experience of each poem as part of a book.

Let's switch analogies. When we talk about our personal space as human beings, we are talking about proxemics. Proxemics is the study of how humans use our bodies in physical space in ways that produce behavior, including verbal and nonverbal social interaction. Intimate distance, for instance, is generally reserved for romantic or sexual partnerships, parent-child relationships, and medical examinations. Public distance, on the other hand, is what we experience in the lecture hall or the park. Consider the relatively standardized behavior of people in the confined space of an elevator in the United States. If someone is alone, that person is likely to stand near the middle, and if a second person gets on, the first tends to move to a corner. As the space fills, everyone turns to face the doors, trying to avoid eye contact and maintain an accepted social distance of arm's length, both for their own comfort and as a courtesy to others. Proxemics, then, is a way to understand relationships among physical–social human bodies in the material world.

Though not perfectly analogous, I propose that the proxemics of poetry is a way to understand how poems function together in the material and conceptual space that is a book. While the conventions of the physical or digital book tend to establish a relatively standardized physical relationship among poems (e.g., poems are titled, each poem begins on a new page, font type and size remain relatively consistent, perhaps there are sections), relationships among one poem and others in a manuscript are not merely a result such material design conventions. Despite material standardization, there exists no agreed-upon organizational standard a poet might easily adopt or adapt. Instead, how poems behave and interact depends on how a book is designed conceptually—which poems belong, how they are ordered, how and when elements repeat, and so on. If we consider the book to be a conceptual—as well as material—space in which poems are socializing, then ordering and cohesion work together as crucial qualities of a book. Something akin to social proximity and distance among poems allows them to be in conversation with each other and shapes those conceptual interactions in various ways.

That's not to say that every poetry book must be overtly or tightly unified, for that risks the sort of forced confinement that works in an elevator only because the trip is short. It's tough to sustain intimate distance for long; such a manuscript can feel uncomfortable or small. But without cohesion—a sense of wholeness, a sense of belonging or interaction—it's tough to sustain the reader's attention across an entire book. In fact, the mere materiality that puts poems into the same space called a book makes it difficult to create a reading experience that is entirely of poem and poem and poem, just as it is difficult to look at a bouquet as flower and flower and flower. In other words, part of why I argue that poetic proxemics exists, is what I call poetic propinquity, or the tendency for readers to discern relationships among poems based on their proximity with each other. As a result, a little cohesion goes a long way in creating just enough but not too much social distance in a poetry book.

In 2003, Beth Ann Fennelly wrote about the rise of the first-book contest and the resulting winnowing of stylistic variety within first collections. There, she points to her own experience, which echoes mine, of submitting her manuscript *Open House* and getting the occasional finalist nod, all the while trying "to sculpt a more directive order, adding new poems when they seemed to provide structure, taking out the most stylistically extreme." She worked toward a level of social distance in which all the poems clicked with seemingly magical connection. Indeed, the epiphany that led me to the sense my first book manuscript was finally really a book involved what Fennelly claims poets did not used to need to do: "give their books a leading title, recurring symbols, and overarching narrative beginning with suffering and ending with redemption." That's not to suggest that these practices are tricks, nor that doing these things can disguise lesser poems inside thematic unification. No, these are techniques that, when used well, can heighten effects of existing propinquity. Of course, even this doesn't ensure a manuscript will be published, and not all published books use these particular organizational techniques. Yet, the choice to use these techniques are among many decisions that create a book's breadth and depth as well as its sense of wholeness.

Though Fennelly worries about the winnowing of wildness, she admits "a pleasure derived from the fullness of a well-developed project, the novelistic depth that be achieved with a tighter focus, the confidence and psychological comfort we feel as readers in the hands of a writer with a stable, practiced voice." This sense that everything fits, clicks, or belongs in a given poetry book involves style, form, and content, and this wholeness ultimately emerges from social distance and proximity among poems.

In her essay "Keeping Company: Thoughts on Arranging Poems," Maggie Anderson, the editor for my first full-length collection, writes of recognizing cohesion in a batch of just thirteen of her own poems. That's when she knows she's working on a book. When she can see repeated sounds, images, nouns, or forms, she contends, "Repetition starts me on assembling a manuscript, and it is this I will attend to most closely at the last stages of putting a book together, as I check for repetitiousness." Manuscript cohesion, then, is affinity but not to the extent of repetitiousness. Importantly, while similarities can play a role, affinity doesn't depend on similarity. Instead, the poetry book as a literary form allows the sense of inclination and aversion, association and distinction.

Likewise, Katrina Vandenberg suggests record albums and the mix tape offer ways to consider poem relationships. Of Ellen Bass's recent book—about what theme? love and marriage? dailiness? compassion?—Patricia Smith writes, "*Indigo* is our soundtrack, finally, with its addictive and merciless music." Does this imply a cohesion through voice? Perhaps a particular *I* and a particular *you,* and, in Bass's words, "how even touch itself cannot mean the same for both of us"? "You can create cohesion in a manuscript," Vandenberg asserts, "by linking poems not just according to the obvious issues of theme, chronology, or similar forms, but also by repeated images, colors, and shapes. You can juxtapose." Juxtaposition, in fact, seems crucial to my concept of the proxemics of poetry because it invites association, and in organizing a manuscript, the poet plays with the possibilities in this type of propinquity. Done poorly, repeated images or forms become tedious, as if a song is being performed by one cover band after another. It's too much of one thing, or it's too much the same too close or, if we consider pacing, too quickly. Exercised deftly, however, techniques of repetition can create a sense of wholeness, an interconnectedness that is not easily defined, other than by example, by the thing itself in practice. Moreover, repetition can delineate dissimilarity and variety by providing a frame of reference beyond a single poem.

One cohesive book that I have taught several times and about which I've also written critically is Natasha Trethewey's *Bellocq's Ophelia.* These poems emerged after Trethewey was introduced, as a student, to the photographs of prostitutes that E. J. Bellocq had taken in the early twentieth century. Based on these surprisingly domestic photographs, Trethewey imagined the character of Ophelia as a light-skinned black woman who moves from Mississippi to New Orleans and ends up working at Countess P—'s "high-class house," where Ophelia is renamed Violet. One section consists of fourteen letter-poems that Ophelia writes, and another section is ten sonnet-like diary-entry poems of fourteen lines. There are a few poems that are not in Ophelia's voice: the opening poem from the perspective of a speaker looking at a particular photograph to see its compositional connection with John Millais's painting of Shakespeare's Ophelia, the poem giving advice in Countess P—'s voice, the poem that describes another particular Bellocq photograph, and the closing poem that imagines the scene of Bellocq taking the book's cover photograph and the woman then "a moment later—after / the flash, blinded—stepping out / of the frame, wide-eyed, into her life." Throughout, terminology and metaphor are drawn from photography. This collection, then, is a dexterously organized, novelistic book that brings to life an imagined character. Readers become immersed in the world of this character, in part as a result of social proximity—and varying distances—among poems within sections and across the book's story. *Bellocq's Ophelia* is designed, in part, as a continuous narrative even though each poem stands on its own too and some sections have their own type of group propinquity

Barbie Chang is another collection that, like Trethewey's, not only brings a character to life but also comments on our cultural moment and history. As the poems' titles suggest, Barbie Chang parks, runs, shakes, can't stop watching, gets her hair done, loves evites, vows to quit, and so on. These poems are connected not only by Barbie Chang but also by a distinctive voice and a syntactical style without punctuation. In an interview in *The Adroit Journal,* poet Victoria Chang says, "I enjoyed word play in *The Boss* and *Barbie Chang* because it was fun and it made writing poetry fun for me. [...] I allowed the language to propel the poems forward instead of me trying to control what they were doing." The cohesive conceit of the character created openness and unpredictability in a writing process led by language. The last of the four sections consists of seven "Dear P." poems that incorporate white spaces within the lines—pauses? pivots? personal space between phrases? Chang says of these poems, "I 'wrote in' those poems after the manuscript was finished— meaning the middle Dear P. poems were from an old manuscript and I felt that there needed to be more Dear P. poems at the end.

But they needed to be different with caesuras and should feel more alight and haunting. So I wrote all of those in section four when the book was mostly done." That addition played with and against existing proxemics in creating the book's cohesion.

Chang's next book, *Obit,* is largely a series she wrote after her mother's death and hearing about a documentary by that name. She told *Kenyon Review,* "I loved that word and I went home and after two weeks had written seventy-five of these." These poems appear as narrow columns with justified margins, like obituaries in the newspaper. The form visually suggests cohesion even if the reader merely flips through the pages without reading for meaning. In addition, these poems form a narrative arc that represents Chang's own chronological working through various effects of loss. "I actually mostly left the poems in the order in which they were written," she said in the same interview, "because I wanted to maintain the integrity of the exploration of grief. Not to get mathematical or anything, but the order of operations was important to me during this process. [...] In which order does grief come?" That's not to say that manuscript cohesion is easily achieved by keeping the poems in the order they were written but that, in this case, the poet's awareness and valuing of proxemics—in chronology of composition, in formatting, in voice—created an organizational strategy and conceptual space early on in the process of writing. Not that Chang had the term *proxemics* in mind but, rather, that she's thoughtful about interactions among poems.

In an interview at *Literary Mama,* Karen Craigo, author of *Welcome to Humansville,* talks of her process in somewhat similar ways: "I give myself projects and I give myself breaks, basically. [...] The projects have such focus and energy, and the breaks let me regroup, sometimes recover, sometimes recalibrate. That's my process, and if I've learned anything over a very herky-jerky writing career, it's that I should trust my process, or at least listen to what it's trying to teach me." Cohesion, then, is a quality of the poetry book that emerges from the writing and revising process as well as a reader's perception based on the type of propinquity at work. As a result, a book often creates a sense of about-ness that we shouldn't dismiss. When I mentioned to a workshop leader at a well-known writers' conference that my recent poems might be part of a larger project, her response was horror over the term *project,* and any interest in my writing or respect she had for me as a writer seemed to vanish. The sense of about-ness I was articulating by using the term *project*, however, doesn't squelch originality, aesthetic integrity, or any given poem's poem-ness or potential. Instead, the conceptual space of a book offers a place for poetic flourishing, a place for poems to socialize with each other.

Other recent project books include Maureen Alsop's *Mantic,* in which each poem explores a type of divination and experiments with language; Lauren Camp's *One Hundred Hungers,* about a first-generation Arab-American girl, diaspora, and assimilation; Oliver de la Paz's *The Boy in the Labyrinth,* about parenting neurodiverse children; Kimiko Hahn's *Foreign Bodies,* a sort of cabinet of curious objects inspired by a collection at the Mütter Museum; Allison Joseph's *Confessions of a Barefaced Women,* a coming-of-age story of a woman of my own generation with life experiences different than my own; Ilya Kaminsky's *Deaf Republic,* a parable about the townspeople of and violence in the imagined Vasenka; Adrian Metejka's *Smoke,* which reimagines the life and myth of boxer Jack Johnson; Hai-Dang Phan's *Reenactments,* which explores family and cultural history and includes translations of work by other Vietnamese poets; Jessica Piazza's *Interrobang,* in which each poem is titled for a phobia or obsession and wordplay abounds; Paisley Rekdal's *Nightingale,* with its retellings of Ovid's *Metamorphosis;* Valerie Wallace's *House of McQueen,* which explores the career and creations of fashion designer Alexander McQueen; and my own second full-length book, *Aperture,* which delves into the lives of real and imagined women and in which I conscientiously explored potential limits of cohesion. Each of these dozen recent books—and certainly many, many others—establishes a relatively well-defined conceptual space, though my brief descriptions don't capture a reader's rich experience.

Cohesion, of course, can work in various ways and is not merely a book's about-ness. Lynn Pedersen's *The Nomenclature of Small Things* draws more directly from science than my own first book, *Constituents of Matter,* which I thought cohered almost entirely around science but which I realized only after it was published was far more autobiographically cohesive. Mathematician-physicist-philosopher Isaac Newton and biologist Charles Darwin show up in Pedersen's book, but so do biblical Eve and painter Johannes Vermeer's woman in blue. In *The Nomenclature of Small Things*, there is no single subject or point but, instead, as Pedersen writes in the poem "A Catalog of What We're Not Meant to See," the sense of "satisfaction or completion just / around the corner or under the pillows / or between the floorboards, something / escaping us in the wind."

In fact, that may be the way cohesion works in most collections that are considered more or less unified. One needn't ever think of a poetry book as a project in order for cohesion to function as a quality we recognize when we read it, even as it is always escaping from our mental grasp just as we are figuring it out. It becomes something we think we know. And then it's not that—or not exactly what we thought. It's more. Though it might seem counterintuitive for me to claim, cohesion builds into the manuscript both sureness and surprise as the gist is dropped, picked up again, recast, transformed. That's accomplished in large part by social distance among poems so that a reader learns how to navigate the unfamiliar space of each book. Social distance and interaction allow readers to find their ways through the conceptual space, even as we each may read our own individual way through.

Let's take Layli Long Soldier's *Whereas* as an example of the relationship of such wayshowing and wayfinding, two concepts

I've borrowed from the field of design. Part II of *Whereas* shares its section title with the book. Titles can work overtly, like directional signs in an unfamiliar airport—we're going to *whereas,* and the structure of the book offers means to get there. The subsection "Whereas Statements," which responds to the "Congressional Resolution of Apology to Native Americans," is especially cohesive, with each of the twenty poems beginning with the word *whereas* in all caps. Repetition is a poetic technique that heightens our wayfinding skills as we both notice and interpret. In an interview with Krista Tibbets, Long Soldier says of this series, "…I felt like this was a project of constraints. So when I sat down to work on this response, there were a lot of constraints that I placed on myself. And one of those was that I wanted all of the pieces to be written, number one, through first person, 'I.' But number two, all of them had to be within living memory. I did not want to jump back 100 years." The interconnectedness of these poems is greater than a reader might consciously notice or be able to articulate, which is part of the brilliance and beauty of cohesion. This quality allows the reader both to be shown the way and also to find the way through the book. In fact, proxemics is at work even when we read out of order.

Part II is not the end-all and be-all of how *Whereas* holds together. The third poem, entitled "Three," consists of four unpunctuated lines formatted on the page as the outline of a square. There's no other poem formally like it in this book. Cohesiveness allows for variance, whether in form, subject matter, or voice. Some poems in *Whereas* are right justified, others are centered, many are conventionally left justified, and some are justified on both margins. Some are single spaced, others are double spaced, and others use unconventional spacing or symbols to separate parts. One ends with a mirror-image of a word, another uses strike-through text, another has text blacked out, and a couple use boxes. There's so much formal experimentation that these surprises end up in conversation with each other—have their own sort of propinquity—and thereby contribute to the book's sureness and interconnectedness as much as to its surprise of form and challenges to literary or textual conventions.

While not the driving force, form and formatting contribute to cohesion—to the experience of the book as a book—in collections like Rachel Eliza Griffith's *Seeing the Body,* torrin a. greathouse's *Wound from the Mouth of a Wound,* Donika Kelly's *The Renunciations,* and Rosebud Ben-Oni's *If This Is the Age We End Discovery.* Griffith, who is also an accomplished photographer, includes several black-and-white self-portrait photographs that, as poet Patricia Smith says, "amplify the lyric as the poet contemplates the world beyond absence." The poet is there in *Seeing the Body*; the reader can actually see her framed in various spaces and imagine her speaking as *I*. And while the speaker's dead mother is absent in one sense, the poems have everything to do with that absence, so that grief becomes a presence that is also that absence.

Wound from the Mouth of a Wound includes a couple of blackout erasure poems, paragraph poems, poems with gaps of white space in the lines, and a poem with a line down the middle. Regardless of or in addition to any topical or thematic interactions, these poems in their formal, structure, or visual variety contribute to the sense of the book's conceptual—or social—space. They orient and organize the experience of reading greathouse's book. Likewise, Kelly's book includes blackout erasure poems titled "Dear—," each of which begins a section, and there are other "Dear—"poems across the collection that are not erasure. As a result, a reader who flips through without even reading yet is likely to sense order or organization. While it doesn't use erasure, Ben-Oni's collection has numerous poem titles that begin with "Poet Wrestling," suggesting a motif. Indented stanzas and lines sprawling over some of the pages embody particular movements within the boundaries of the physical and conceptual space of this book. An organizing force is evident, even as it is difficult to label.

What of a book that isn't a project and adheres to traditional justification and spacing? Is a book of poems ever merely a bunch of poems? Based on humans' propensity for propinquity, I would argue no, a book is a book is a book even if it is a bunch of poems. As poets and also as readers, we tend to find cohesion, which is not to say we impose it so much as putting poems together necessarily creates interactions among them. Some might argue that all poems written by a given poet would naturally have connections to each other, but poets also experiment and change over time. Even if everything a poet writes is of a piece regardless of the poet's range, understanding the book as a book—as a poetic form, as a reading experience—urges us to consider proxemics as part of the way meaning is made.

In the examples I've discussed, cohesion is not an on-or-off quality, and there's no one way to recognize or achieve it. A poet—or a reader—might create a word cloud to visualize the weight of repeated words and to discern dominant ideas and then play with these words, ideas, and variations. Or the word cloud may make clear repetitiousness or thematic oversimplification that undermines the work. A poet or reader might read aloud the last line of one poem and the first line of the next, looking only at juxtapositions and linkages—indications of social interactions or propinquity—from poem to poem. The poet or reader might ask, which poem is too far afield conceptually to hear another's poem's question and respond, and which poem is so close to others that it steps on their toes? I feel as if I'm nearing the appropriate level of cohesion when I both can see a gap where a new poem might belong (where the social distance is much greater than arm's length) and can tell which poems need to be moved (need more elbow room) or removed (are in the wrong room).

Anderson says, "The poems inside a single collection must keep each other company." Too much intimacy risks poems circling so tightly—perhaps forced to do so, as if in an elevator—that if you've read one, you've read them all. These poems suffer from cabin fever; they're anxious, or they're bored with each other. They need some room to breathe or relax, to do their thing. Yet, excessive expansiveness can leave interaction indiscernible. Some poems are wandering off; they've missed the boat or taken a long walk off a short pier as they lose track of their surroundings. Each poem demands its own space, but the manuscript or the book is not an infinite or empty space.

The proxemics of poetry offers ways to examine these relationships and suggests how the art and craft of any single-author poetry collection—or anthology, for that matter—works in practice, even when the reader doesn't read start to finish in order. Proxemics is a tool, if you like that metaphor for craft or for criticism, as much as it is a phenomenology of poetry books. Whereas materiality forms the physical book and includes wayshowing and wayfinding cues, proxemics describes the book's bookness. What's most amazing to me about the notion of the proxemics of poetry is that it explains how a poem can be itself fully—have its individual meaning and effect—and also be fully part of a larger composition that comes into being on its own terms.

Previously published in *The Writer's Chronicle*.

Improvising Order

~Vivian Wagner

I've been writing a poem each day, using prompts from *The Daily Poet: Day-by-Day Prompts for Your Writing Practice,* by Kelli Russell Agodon and Martha Silano, for several years. It's been a valuable practice, and the sheer number of poems it's helped me to create is comforting. It's like having food in the pantry, or money in the bank. I have a storehouse.

When putting together a collection a while back, I looked through my files full of poems inspired by *The Daily Poet* prompts. I organize my poems by month and year, and I realized I had some themes going on. I hadn't planned these themes, and I hadn't thought of them ahead of time. But they were there. I found parenting poems and mountain poems, cat poems and tree poems. Nearly every poem, in fact, had at least several counterparts, whispering of shared narratives and obsessions and interests.

The parenting theme, in particular, seemed promising. Without consciously realizing it, I'd written a number of poems about what it means to be a mother, to have been a child, and I started realizing that maybe there was, in fact, a collection waiting to be put together. I started going through the poems one by one, saving all the ones that had anything to do with parenting or childhood in their own folder. I discovered that, indeed, there were more than enough for a collection. I played with them for a while, experimenting with possible organizational principles. I wanted the poems to speak to each other, so I grouped ones about my kids when they were teenagers and when they became young adults, and I also grouped together ones about my own childhood. Before long I had a collection called *Raising* on my hands, and it was published in 2018 by Clare Songbirds Publishing House.

What I discovered in this process is that sometimes a collection's order can be improvised with whatever materials you have on hand. Sometimes, you don't plan ahead for a collection's theme— it just happens, growing organically out of the work you create. If you write enough poems, in other words, you're almost certain to eventually have a thematic collection on your hands. It's just a matter of trusting the process, giving it time, letting your work breathe and age, and finally looking objectively and with an editor's eye at what you've produced. In this way, you can make sense out of even a seemingly non-thematic daily practice. The poems we create almost automatically have a theme, in other words, if only because we're the ones creating them. We're the common denominator. We're the theme.

How can order be improvised? It's a process similar to any other kind of improvisation. When you don't know what to cook for dinner but don't want to go shopping, for instance, you look in the refrigerator and the cupboard, see what you have, and come up with a plan. You make it up on the fly. Improvising means taking stock of a moment or situation, and then doing what you can with what's available. There's always meaning to be made. There's always something to be done.

I first started thinking about improvisation when I was learning to fiddle and working on a book about fiddling. I was raised as a classical violinist, always playing by the rules and following the music on the page. When as an adult I started learning to fiddle, however, I discovered there was a whole world of improvising, and I fell in love with it. When improvising, you might start with a melody or a chord, but then you work within and around those basic elements and create something entirely new. As Pauline Oliveros says in "Quantum Improvisation: The Cybernetic Presence," "the improvising musician has to let go of each moment and also simultaneously understand the implications of any moment of the music in progress as it emerges into being" (121). It's almost a mystical experience to trust in this emergence. The moment of creation always can and will happen. I realized as

I was learning to fiddle that the skill of improvising is valuable in many other situations, as well. When getting divorced, for instance, or raising children. Or putting together poetry collections.

In her book, *Improv Wisdom: Don't Prepare, Just Show Up*, which is about the connections between improv and life, Patricia Ryan Madson says that "improvising invites us to lighten up and look around. It offers an alternative to the controlling way many of us try to lead our lives" (20). Improv, she argues, involves letting go of expectations and learning to trust the process of creation. As she says, "improv points to ways of being more and better alive, ways of cutting through our patterns of procrastination and doubt" (147). We tend to think that to make something, we must first know what we're going to create. In my experience as both a musician and a writer, however, I've learned that not knowing what we're doing—at least at first—can be the greatest gift we can give ourselves. Sometimes our best creations come about when we trust the process and let go of our desire to control what happens.

This isn't to say that a collection and a theme might well come about through a conscious decision-making process long before the writing of any individual poem. It's just to say that sometimes, if we just show up each morning and create something, anything, those pieces could start to adhere, to speak to one another, to express larger, broader, or deeper meanings that might not have been obvious to us at first. And from those seemingly disconnected pieces, a collection can be born.

Be Kind to Yourself

Interview with Claudia Castro Luna

DtM: In this ever-growing poetry world, with so many poets publishing books, what makes for an outstanding poetry manuscript?

CCL: A manuscript that stays consistent to a vision from beginning to end. By this I mean that the craft choices the writer made throughout are in service of this vision and that by the time the reader reads the last poem there is a sense of discovery, a resonance of feeling or understanding that the language conveyed. There is also the pure delight of language that has to be present in any manuscript.

DtM: What trick or technique have you learned in ordering your poetry book that could help someone put their first poetry book together?

CCL: Print the entire manuscript. Read the poems out loud to yourself. Look for reverberations: rhythmic, content, sound. Are you leaning into a particular image? Are you fond of a particular syntactical twist? Do you repeat a word/words? This exercise will make patterns evident and the author can then decide if the patterns discovered are by design and should therefore remain in the manuscript, or if it would be better to change them somehow. Being aware of tendencies and patterns and how they are serving, or detracting from, the manuscript is crucial.

DtM: If you could give a poet a few words of advice in creating their poetry manuscript, what would that advice be?

CCL: Be kind to yourself. Poems take time to reach full expression. There are exceptions of course. But for the most part I would say that allowing distance between the poet and the poem is a very good thing. Let a poem live on its own for a few weeks, in a folder, inside a drawer. When you return to it, if it reads exactly as you heard it in your head when you last touched it, then it is close. I don't know that there is ever the sense that a poem is 100% complete. We do need to let go of them at some point but rushing through the writing is not useful. Returning to a poem allows us to see it with fresh eyes and ears. We may catch a rhyme, a word, a line break that is not vibrating quite like we wish it to be. This is the moment to do exquisite revisions or to return to the drawing table. Listening closely to the poem, the writer will know if more work needs to be done.

DtM: What do you know now about creating a manuscript, as you work on your third book?

CCL: I understand manuscripts as following two trends. The first is a manuscript where the poems are written and collected over time, their fulcrum is the writer, her interests, thematically and craft wise. I am thinking here of Denise Levertov's work for instance.

Another type of manuscript is the one born from a discreet thematic choice: to explore a divorce such as Sharon Olds does in *Stag's Leap*, to investigate a town's history as Mark Nowak does in *Revenants* or to pry open a disaster as Patricia Smith does in *Blood Dazzler*.

I have a lot more clarity now about which type of manuscript I would like to put my energies into. Of the two types above I lean into the second kind. Having clarity about the overall thrust of the manuscript helps me hone the craft choices will best support my new exploration.

Persistence, Persistence, Persistence

Interview with Greg Santos

DtM: In this ever-growing poetry world, with so many poets publishing books, what makes for an outstanding poetry manuscript?

GS: The more you write, the more your writing muscles will flex. Don't be afraid to experiment and play. Speak your truth, whatever that may be. No one else can tell your story or write the way you do, so the more confident your voice, the more your poetry manuscript will stand out.

DtM: What trick or technique have you learned in ordering your poetry book that could help someone put their first poetry book together?

GS: My most recent poetry book, *Ghost Face* (DC Books), is divided into three different sections. Now that I reflect on it, all my full-length poetry books are divided that way. Why the number three? I am not sure why. As a kid, three was always a lucky number. I have found that listening to your gut feeling when something feels right is the way to go.

But I also feel like separating my book into different sections (1. I/You 2. Saudade 3. Ode to Joy) helps connect and group poems that explore similar themes, subjects, and ideas. For instance, the "I/You" poems touch on identity: trying to make sense of being a transracial adoptee with Khmer ancestry who was raised by Canadian parents. The "Saudade" section features poems centred on hauntings, mourning, and memory. While "Ode to Joy" features more funny, playful, and hopeful pieces, which I found a nice way to finish off the book.

Except for many of the poems in the "I/You" section, most of the poems in *Ghost Face* were originally written as standalone pieces. It was only once I started putting the manuscript together that I began to see how certain poems played off one another, with words, images, and themes being built up to what I hope is an elegiac crescendo.

So, while you might not have a specific book project in mind, when you start piecing a manuscript together, pay attention to how your poems talk to one another. You might just end up surprised by the word magic that can occur when seemingly different poems are juxtaposed with each other.

DtM: If you could give a poet a few words of advice in creating their poetry manuscript, what would that advice be?

GS: When you have enough poems to put together a full-length manuscript (based on my experience that means 48 poems or more), find a person who you feel comfortable sharing your writing with. Not everyone has the privilege of having a mentor or an editor but having a peer or someone whose opinions you trust can be so valuable to an emerging writer. Having that extra set of eyes on your work can be beneficial in gaining a reader's perspective on what your poems read like.

DtM When your first book came into the world, could you describe the mixture of emotions this book entails for you? Can you describe your journey?

GS: My first full-length poetry book, *The Emperor's Sofa*, started off as my creative thesis for my MFA at The New School. After I graduated, I was enthusiastic and started sending off my poetry manuscript out to presses, contests, and publishing houses. That was in the Fall of 2009. I received numerous rejections, but I plugged away and remained persistent. If anything, I learned that you must really believe in your work.

It wasn't until Spring 2010 that Montreal poet and scholar, Jason Camlot, whose writing I greatly admired, contacted me to inquire whether my manuscript, which I had sent back in the fall, was still available. I was thrilled when Camlot informed me that he was interested in working with me to edit it for Montreal's storied DC Books, which was founded by Louis Dudek and his wife, Aileen Collins in 1974. The first book DC published was *Dk/ Some Letters of Ezra Pound*, a collection of letters between Dudek and Ezra Pound.

I recall that it was a particularly poignant time for me: I had been offered a new teaching job and our first child was born that year. I was proud, nervous, excited, and found it extremely hard to be patient. Ultimately, when my debut book, *The Emperor's Sofa*, was published in December of 2010, it really did feel like a dream come true. Ten years later, I am so pleased to have three full-length poetry collections under my belt with DC Books.

Let Each Rejection Encourage You to Go Deeper

Interview with Su Hwang

DtM: In this ever-growing poetry world, with so many poets publishing books, what makes for an outstanding poetry manuscript?

SW: As writers and readers, we have our own preferences, come from diverse backgrounds, resonate with different voices. All to say: everything is subjective. As a writer of color and daughter of immigrants, I struggled for most of my life thinking I had to conform or fit into certain boxes established by the white canon and its attendant gatekeepers. Thankfully this notion has shifted dramatically in the last few years because, like language and nature, the "canon" is ever-evolving, transmuting, blooming. Slowly but surely, more and more marginalized voices are getting their due, so the more poetry in the world, I believe, the better.

As a reader, I seek out collections that blend awe with craft, with soul—whether it contends with the personal, social, spiritual, ecological, or astral. It's thrilling when I can immerse myself in a poetry collection from cover to cover, be totally consumed by its language, sounds, imagery, and the emotions it evokes. I tend to gravitate toward work that tells an authentic story, tapping into the universal at both the macro and micro spheres through innovation of form and/or perspective. Collections that stay with me usually blow my mind open, altering it somehow while making it whole again. Show me something reimagined or point me toward a special thread of possibility. I mean, that's the best we can do as writers. The rest is out of our control in terms of how the work is read or received on the other end. Don't write what you think others want to read; write what you are, where you've been, and where you want to go. Let the reader journey with you. And because art is subjective, we need more and more of it.

DtM: What trick or technique have you learned in ordering your poetry book that could help someone put their first poetry book together?

SH: For two years, after defending my MFA thesis as a late bloomer in poetry, I went through dozens and dozens of manuscript iterations—trials and many errors. An MFA provides time to read and experiment, but it doesn't teach you how to organize a poetry manuscript per se. Given that this was my first collection, I really had no idea what I was doing, and unfortunately, there is no one-size-fits-all formula for these things. By a stroke of good fortune, I crossed paths with master poet Rick Barot, who offered generous, invaluable advice and inspired a dark night of the soul kind of final revision. He told me to cut twenty-five pages, go back to three sections instead of five, and suggested new opening and closing poems. I realize not everyone has access to someone like Rick Barot, but finding a mentor or reader you trust, even if it means saving up a little money to compensate them for their time and labor, can dramatically shift the trajectory of a manuscript. Be open to constructive criticism. Our kneejerk reaction as writers may be defensiveness, but finding detachment can offer up even greater expansion. Writing a manuscript can veer toward obsession, if done well in my opinion, so it's useful to get feedback from someone with a bit of distance since we all have our blind spots. Even if you disagree with another reader's reflections, you can at least have a conversation about it and concretize your own ideas, or perhaps a nugget of wisdom will kickstart new ways to consider the manuscript. Writing is a solitary act, but getting your work published, well, that takes a village.

For the *Chicago Review of Books*, I was invited to offer my thoughts on how the last poem in my book was selected (I basically elaborate on what Rick Barot told me), along with poets Natalie Diaz, Leah Huizar, and Kimberly Quiogue Andrews regarding their respective collections, and I found their wisdom and insights to be invaluable. The interviews were part of a feature series edited by writer Sarah Blake, on how several poets put together their manuscripts from choosing their titles to their opening poems. I highly recommend checking out this online series as another handy resource to get fresh ideas. Since the publication of my book, I've helped a few friends reshuffle their manuscripts to positive results and their first poems were all buried somewhere in the manuscript. If you're feeling stuck with your manuscript, I'd venture to guess you need a new starting point, which will invariably alter your last poem and everything in between. And if all else fails, a celebrated poet friend once suggested: "When in doubt, always start with death."

DtM: If you could give a poet a few words of advice in creating their poetry manuscript, what would that advice be?

SH: Rejection is an integral part of the process, so try not to be paralyzed by it. It stings like hell, but remember, art is subjective. I know it's easier said than done, but let each rejection encourage you to go even deeper. For a while, I printed my rejection letters and taped them to a wall like a loony sadist. This particular motivational technique might not be for everyone, but try to frame each "no" as an opportunity to improve the work, to fire you up, to keep chipping away as if you're sculpting marble. Be meticulous, exacting. Writing is 20% creative spark, 80% revision, in my opinion. For nearly two years, I worked on a version of the collection every single day, whether it was overhauling the structure holistically, or as Oscar Wilde put it, "I spent most of the day putting in a comma and the rest of the day taking it out." In fact, I was tweaking the manuscript until my publisher sent the file to the printer. There was always something I could reconsider, revise, revitalize. Without going mad, commit to looking at the manuscript on a daily basis from a birds-eye view or with a microscope—make it a healthy obsession. At some point, it should become fun, as if you're putting together a moving target of a puzzle. It also helped that during the two years I was submitting and revising the manuscript, I was also developing a spiritual practice. For me, this was learning about ancient

Hellenistic astrology, reading tarot, and other esoteric systems. If possible, find other healthy obsessions to take the edge off of working on the manuscript.

As for submitting, be sure the first few poems in your manuscript are pristine, airtight. If you have sections in the manuscript, bookend them with your strongest pieces. Find a friend to proofread. Don't use strange fonts. Having been a first-round reader for a national poetry contest, I can tell you that small details matter. Since I was only able to move forward a couple of manuscripts from nearly a hundred submissions, any reason to pass just made my task easier. If a manuscript didn't pull me in from the first few poems or it was laden with avoidable bobbles, I moved on. Because most poetry debuts are contest-based, sadly, you really only get one chance to make a great first impression. And remember, art is subjective, so don't compare yourself to another writer's journey. The handful of manuscripts I passed on to the next round in that contest might have been totally different if that batch were assigned to another reader.

DtM: Your first book has recently come into the world! Can you describe the mixture of emotions this book entails for you? Can you describe your journey?

SH: It's kind of a long story best told over several conversations and drinks or tea probably, but my journey has been a circuitous one, with plenty of dead ends and detours to boot. I was forty-five years old when my debut collection was published in late 2019, after a series of rejections and near misses, and decades crippled by a very obnoxious inner critic and a debilitating fear of failure. Looking back, I don't think I would change a thing, enriched by all the trials and tribulations, as well as experiences, friendships, and small victories over many years, but I also realize hindsight is an easier pill to swallow. This particular passage from Kim Addonizio's *Ordinary Genius*, which happens to be on my homepage, continues to resonate: "Before wanting to be a poet I did many things: worked hateful low-paying jobs, lived in a lot of group houses, took up the flute, read, drank, took drugs, found my way in and out of friendships and love relationships. My life didn't change once I discovered poetry. But I had found my direction. I didn't have a great aptitude—my early poems were truly terrible—but I had a calling at last. I realized that poetry was my gift. My 'genius.'"

Something tectonic within definitely shifts after publishing a first book. There was a huge cathartic release from the psychic weight I've been carrying for most of my life, perhaps even ancestral trauma. For a few months, I could silence that pesky inner critic and feel like I made my parents and friends proud. I still pinch myself because there were decades when I didn't think this was remotely possible, and I continue to be filled with gratitude when a reader connects with the work. But there are many aspects of daily life that remain the same after the first book: you still have to get up every day, cook food, do the dishes, walk the dog, take out the trash, pay the bills. The book you publish might be on blast for a few months on social media, garner some good reviews, maybe even win a nice award if you're lucky, but time doesn't stop and new books come and go. Yes, publishing a first book allows for new opportunities and contacts, but I think it's important to focus on the making of art. External trappings only feed the ego and are fleeting; peace of mind comes from feeding the soul. No doubt publishing a book is an amazing achievement, so I don't want to diminish its joyful aspects, but if poetry is a calling then it's a lifelong pursuit, not a flash in the pan. I think it's essential to remain grounded and to keep doing the work, even if it means staring at the wall full of rejection letters. There's an old Zen saying: "Before enlightenment, chop wood and carry water. After enlightenment, chop wood and carry water." Replace enlightenment with "publishing" for the same application, because as I stare at the empty pages of my next collection, we all begin again, anew.

The Poetry Collection is a Place for Disparities, Or Let It Bleed

~Jennifer Givhan

When I originally compiled my first collection *Landscape with Headless Mama*, I imagined the book very differently, called it *Red Sun Mothers*, and divided it into sections based on the experiences of different mother-entities in Mexican/American culture, including the infertile woman (or adoptive mother) and the psychologically-socially unstable mother (La Llorona—Mexican Medea figure). I began the collection before I adopted my son, and it was published when he was nine years old, so it was in flux all those years. And as the collection progressed while I raised my children, I realized the divisions were not so clearly delineated. Even after becoming a mother, sometimes the grief of miscarriage seeped through, and even in joy, there was also exhaustion and uncertainty, which sometimes gave way to fear and anxiety-induced mental illness, near breaks with reality, so that La Llorona was never as far from the supposedly stable mother as she might at first seem.

In the meantime, I read contemporary collections that struck deep chords and inspired new ways of seeing the shape of my poems as individuals and together—books like Natasha Trethewey's *Native Guard*, Julia Alvarez's *Homecoming*, Patricia Smith's *Shoulda Been Jimi Savannah*, and Claudia Emerson's *Late Wife*. Reading these collections and then looking back to my own material, I found that my poems showed me how many conflicting desires and facets of truth/experience they could hold at once, how they could negotiate these borderland spaces where nothing is as clearly defined as we might wish—motherhood is messy, and the book showed me how to embrace that via the structure—so that Mama's story bleeds into the speaker's own, and it's never entirely clear whether the speaker is the mother or the daughter. That bleeding uncertainty is purposeful and came after many years of trying structure after structure until I found the perfect one that asked each poem to do multiple layers of work.

Think of your poetry collection as a world, as a landscape, as a city, a room. Think as large or small as you need to for your poems to become as important and personal as they need to be for you to see them as a whole. By this I mean they should each carry a shape, a weight, a specific texture and color and smell within the collection, the way a place or character in your birthplace or childhood hometown would; think back to your street. On mine, Rio Vista, there were date palms, purplish jewels fallen to the dirt lot that separated the neighborhood from a dirt hill that led down to the New River, polluted and toxic carrying waste from the border, forty minutes away, bleeding socio-political alongside the glowing, dying fish.

Each poem in a collection occupies space in this world, and thereby offers up its significance, connected in some tangible way to those residing beside it. In mine: the house I grew up in, the neighbors' houses where I experienced abuses and made lifelong friends, those palm trees dropping those squishy fruits that still remind me of the cockroaches infesting our bathrooms summerlong, the packed-earth hills I slid on my backside to the riverbanks below, where some still believe La Llorona herself haunts, and on those mud-cracked banks, the blood of her children.

See how I've gone from most personal home to most socially-connected river, with its border politics, its cultural myths—but they're interlinked, my home beside that polluted water.

There are any number of ways you could order the space you've created—it's your world, after all. My collections often begin with the most personal and yet I believe the personal is inherently political. In this way, a narrative begins to emerge, and carry with it the undercurrent of deeper troubled waters. I don't recommend you stick only to chronology. I've found that any chronological order that arises in my collections comes after finding deeper and more nuanced connections in the spaces between the poems. For example, in *Landscape with Headless Mama*, chronology came after discovering that Mama and the speaker's stories were interwoven. Then I could tell multiple stories at once. A clear chronology felt too facile; I'd tried that at one point and it didn't feel honest in the way that the imagination can sometimes get at deeper truths than nonfiction. Instead, the chronology in the structure comes from a narrative underpinning. I love story—the power of story. And it was important to me that in telling my own story, I was speaking the truths of my own mother(s)—the women I grew up with in the Imperial Valley and in my own Mexican-American *familia*, even when the stories were nonlinear and messy.

A poetry collection is a place for disparities and oppositions and paradoxes to coexist and coalesce and stretch us to find new ways of existing within the flux. So even your most contentious, paradoxical poems can work together if you're finding how they fit in the larger space. If you cannot find the connections even in the breaking places, then perhaps those poems are not meant for this particular world, and you should save them for another. I've found that poems I took out of my first collection ended up fitting perfectly in my second and beyond. My third collection, for example, retells some of Mama's story but from a new angle, for compiling each collection has required of me stretching and seeing and re-seeing in new ways.

During a manuscript consultation a writer asked me whether or not her poems of being an abused daughter fit in a collection so clearly about a mother caring for a child with special needs. She'd received conflicting advice from her mentor and felt torn about whether or not the differences and breaking places could ever fit together. I said, *absolutely—in the world you've created*. Being a mother is not separate from being a woman. And being a motherwoman is not separate from being a daughtergirl. I've found this over and over in my own life and poems. I've found the most freedom in my work when I've allowed everything to bleed, as I have bled. The past tinges the present, but the strangeness and heart truth is that the present tinges the past. That's been the heartwork of mothering, for me. Mothering poetry and children.

Keep finding ways to coalesce and shed light and shadow on the different angles of your poems and your life, poets. Keep finding places of connection, where that jeweled date falls from palm to dirt—a hinge between the personal and political—write there.

Ruthlessness

~Diana Goetsch

I'm inspired by something the poet John Berryman said to a young Philip Levine: "Be ruthless with your poems, or someone else will be." I've got a sense that ruthlessness, more than talent or skill or inspiration, gives me my best chance of distinguishing myself from my peers, and gives my poems their best chance of being read and remembered.

I don't think Berryman's advice had anything to do with nastiness (though Berryman did some nasty things). It had more to do with love, the love required of a drill sergeant preparing young soldiers for combat, loving them with every barked order—"Get down and give me 10!"—and eliminating the weak ones, who pose a danger to themselves and to the group. Berryman wanted Levine to cultivate standards higher than any critic, so that his poems might stick around.

How does ruthlessness translate to my own work?—how do I make a poem get down and give me 10? One practice I've adopted comes in the beginning of the creative process. If I look at a first draft of a poem and understand everything in it, I'll set it aside as an exercise and never look at it again. That goes especially for when what I've written seems like it's pretty good. I know that feeling from early on in my writing life: "Hey, this is pretty good," I'd tell myself, then show it to a few friends who concurred: pretty good. It *looks* like a poem, it's eminently competent, even smart. And it's a waste of time.

When William Packard once told me that a poem of mine was good, he also said, "You know, the enemy of the great poem isn't the bad poem, it's the good poem." I've since learned that, while bad poems are harmless, in that they would never deceive us, "good" poems are inherently limited and dangerous, in that they were made to please our egos, and are very difficult to come away from. Conversely, if I look at an early draft of a poem and don't quite understand it—can't even tell if it's *good or not*—I know it has a chance, and I become interested in it.

The other thing I require in a new piece of writing is that it bear no resemblance to the last thing I've written, even if the last thing was groundbreaking. Art is demanding: as soon as you break the same ground twice, you're in a rut. How many poets, even well-known ones, wind up writing essentially the same poem, making the same moves, repeatedly? Maybe I'm destined to do this too, but ultimately that's a concern for readers and critics, if I'm fortunate enough to have them. In the meantime, I owe it to myself not to be hoodwinked by the familiar good poem.

Another form of ruthlessness comes at the other end of the creative process, when I'm putting together a manuscript. Periodically, I'll pull up the table of contents on my computer and employ the tab and delete keys like machetes. Any title of a poem that I don't then and there consider top notch, I'll tab over half an inch from the others. I can't tell you right here what "top notch" is—just to say that certain titles cling to the left margin, and others can't, for whatever reason, hold on anymore. They're *asking* to be moved, and I need to listen. These are cousins of the poems from previous books I never read in public, and wish I'd deleted when I had the chance.

Then I look at the poems I've tabbed over half an inch, inspecting for weak wolves in this pack, and I might tab some of *these* over another half inch. So now I have three ranks. The "one-inchers" get deleted—regardless of where they may have already been published. The "half-inchers" might eventually make it, but they need time. The most ruthless move of all is when I decide to wait another year before sending out a manuscript that, earlier in my writing life, I'd be too hungry not to submit. These days I'm hungry for the time to revise some of the "tabbed" poems, and compose some better ones.

All of us have bought poetry books, or record albums for that matter, knowing there's plenty of slack in them. I've got a Sheryl Crow album with two and a half good songs on it, and I don't regret the purchase. It's what most artists do. All the more special, though, when we behold *Pet Sounds* by the Beach Boys, Carole King's *Tapestry*, Bruce Springsteen's *Darkness on the Edge of Town,* or the Beatles' *Abbey Road*. In the world of contemporary poetry, there are those rare collections with zero slack—Galway Kinnell's *Imperfect Thirst* and Stephen Dobyns's *Cemetery Nights* immediately come to mind. And I'm especially inspired by the poets, such as Marie Howe and Jack Gilbert, who have had a capacity to wait, while any number of editors would gladly publish earlier, inferior versions of their volumes.

There are 34 poems in my newest collection. At various points, 31 other poems were included in the manuscript, then subsequently deleted. The collection is called *Nameless Boy*. I'm not claiming it's *Abbey Road,* just that I was able to keep improving it, ruthlessly.

Post Acceptance

Interview with Oliver de la Paz

DtM: What do you wish you knew before beginning the publishing process of each of your books? Feel free to focus on the most recent.

OdlP: With my first book, I honestly had no idea what I didn't know. I was doing as I was told by my advisors and mentors in my MFA program. I had sent to as many poetry contests as I could afford. By the time I had finished my second book of poems, I knew that I didn't want to apply to every contest under the sun and that certain presses had certain styles or voices they preferred. For example, Fence has a particular type of manuscript they're looking for while something like the National Poetry Series had a broader vision based on the diversity of the publishing companies that took in prize winners under the NPS umbrella. Now, I've chosen to stop entering all contests save the NPS. At a certain point in my writing career, I developed a relationship with editors of presses (even those that haven't published my work) by virtue of the continuation of my writing practice which includes publishing in literary journals.

DtM: What is the single most useful thing you have learned about creating a book of poems?

OdlP: I learned that sometimes retyping an entire manuscript from scratch can be beneficial. I found that by retyping all the poems, I could identify places where poems deviated from a particular stylistic leaning, where the syntax moved away from the dominant pattern of the manuscript, and where tonal shifts occurred. Retyping the manuscript was also useful in defining relational organization—how one poem responds to the poems adjacent to it.

DtM: Please describe the process of book creation as it applies to your last book.

OdIP: My book, *Post Subject: A Fable* started as a series of postcards for a month-long poetry postcard exchange with members of Kundiman (a non-profit Asian American literary arts organization) during the summer of 2007. I wrote ekphrastic poems based on the images on the postcard. The address to "Empire" which became the big structuring impulse for the book, occurred three to four postcards into the exchange. Soon after that, I was including the "Dear Empire" address to all of the postcards. After the month ended, I continued to write the epistolary poems.

DtM: What was your process for ordering the poems? Sections? No sections? Tough decisions?

OdIP: At the end of roughly four or five years of writing these "Dear Empire" poem, I had to figure out how to sort through the one-hundred poems that were clearly part of a series. So I assembled them alphabetically. Each poem has a declarative sentence after the address: "This is your road," "These are your signs," etc. I used the noun object at the end of the sentence as the alphabetizing word. After I lived with that organization, I decided that it was too cluttered and unfriendly to general readers, so I kept an alphabetizing mechanism, and implemented sections: "Address," "Atlas," "Ledger," "Zoo," and "Zygote."

The sections "Address" and "Zygote" serve as framing devices and contain only one poem.

The sections "Atlas," "Ledger," and "Zoo" alphabetically contain poems from the catalog and easily fall into categories of poems about geographical features, goods and objects, and animals and people.

I wanted to give the reader a sense that someone was cataloging someone's possessions or that someone was listing assets. Further, I wanted the reader to feel the burden of the catalog.

DtM: How did you choose your title? Cover art? Font? All of those details that come post acceptance! (Or did your publisher have control?)

OdIP: The title came along about two or three years after I started writing the poems. I didn't want to be lazy and title the manuscript "Dear Empire." I wanted, also, to hint at the notion of Post Colonialism and the strangeness of that idea. That's why I added the subtitle "A Fable" to *Post Subject: A Fable*.

I had seen haunting photos of urban ruins in the book, *States of Decay*, and I wanted to have a photo as my cover. Unfortunately, due to copyright issues, I couldn't get anything from the book. So, Amy Freels, the designer at the University of Akron Press, sent along links to Flickr images that fit my idea. We had a lot to choose from and settled on the one that had the most celebratory colors contrasted against the ruin of the setting.

I don't remember having much of a conversation about the font for the book because I had worked with Amy previously on *Requiem for the Orchard*. It was a very smooth process.

Post acceptance, I filled out a very long questionnaire for the publisher to determine the book's marketing. It's a form that should always be taken seriously and some research should be done in terms of determining places to send review copies. I had a list of a few journals and newspapers and developed a few more leads through queries of friends.

DtM: What have we forgotten to ask you?

OdIP: Nowadays, you should always double check on digital rights for books. Make sure that your contract has something about that in place. If it doesn't, ask for it. I'm seeing more and more collections of poetry in e-book form.

Moving Through the Dark: A Poet's Yoga

~Alison Pelegrin

It's dark in the yoga studio for my early morning class. No one can see me, nor I them. No mirrors, and I'm glad, because I'm not graceful, and there's nothing willowy about my body—sometimes I wonder why I come here at all. It's a constant battle for me, in yoga and poetry, to let go of grumpy doubt, and to poke, instead, at the unknown, with a pencil or the tip of my toe.

Keep Your Eyes On Your Mat

Why the great temptation among poets and yogis to worry about what others are doing? When I dwell on the effort I've squandered chasing milestones set by other poets—a book by this age, fellowships by this age, residencies here, poems featured there—it sickens me. It is exhausting to run someone else's race, yet I am always lacing up my shoes. Maintaining a pose or a line of thought is difficult in the best state of mind. Get distracted for an instant by someone in a fancy arm balance or with a pull-out special feature in *Poetry* magazine and you are bound to lose your balance.

Find Your Work

In fourth grade there was a boy who made me believe he could move pencils with his eyes. If he glowered long enough at a tooth-marked number two, it seemed to wobble across the desk and into his lap. I envied the ease with which he performed this magic. And thus, began my writing life: hunched over the desk, a pulsing knot of frustration, while everyone else, it seemed, worked magic with their minds.

I want writing to be easy, and the same goes for publications and books. Still, it's better to renounce the quick fix of easy affirmation and force yourself to find your work—your flood subject. The risk will pay off. Eventually. I submitted to a journal for twenty years before they accepted a poem of mine. For the twentieth anniversary issue.

Honor Yourself

Why is it so difficult to wait for what you know you want? An inability to be patient and to honor my work was one of my biggest mistakes as a young poet. The most painful example involves my first manuscript. Because I did not experience instant success, I lost faith in my poems and said yes to a novice press unequipped to promote and distribute my work. I was so desperate to be a poet with a book that I never considered there could be such a thing as a poet with a bad book.

I still cringe when I see that book, and I wish I had never signed the contract. The manuscript had been a finalist in a few book contests—why didn't anyone tell me to hold out? Why didn't anyone tell me that once a manuscript hits finalist status it's just a matter of time before the work clicks with an editor or judge?

Listen

Sometimes you write poems, and sometimes a vision comes to you in a flash during a prolonged, hurricane-induced exile. It was on one of these uprooted days that the title of my second manuscript came in a fevered, air mattress dream. I put the book together at my kitchen table the first day back in my rebuilt house.

I had been circulating the same, barely tinkered with a group of poems for years. The time I won a book contest, I sent in something new. I remember it as the best day of my life—not the months-later phone call from the press, but the delight of the work of which I was so certain and which spoke so clearly to me . The work sang and I followed. Outside my kitchen window, lumberjacks sliced and dropped the limbs of diseased pine trees, and the poems clicked in place despite the buzz. There were no locks on any of my new, unpainted doors.

Be Honest

I wrote a book-that-almost-wasn't. An editor at a great press asked if I had a manuscript for her. I was lying when I said yes. True, I had a group of poems that I had been working on for a while, true I had a title in mind for what these poems might one day become, but my work was nowhere near finished.

Still, I went through the poet's yoga of spreading pages across the floor and relying on whim instead of instinct to shuffle them into some sort of order, replete with filler poems to make a respectable page count. And this is how I learned that nine months of silence from a press that solicits your work is not a good sign.

Set An Intention

With both my squandered manuscript and my book-that-almost-wasn't, I chased too soon after my intentions. Discernment is part of writing poems, which to me means time spent sitting in silence and considering my intentions. Not the easy, instant, surface intentions, but the ones I may not want to acknowledge, surfacing like monsters from the deep.

On the mat or facing the page, I often can't find an intention. At these times, I say to myself, quoting Goethe, "Do not hurry, do not rest." A perfect wisdom, and also a phrase that could be scripted across tee shirts at the yoga studio.

Take What You Need

Poetry and yoga are all about beginnings. How many times does my attempt at an arm balance end in a face plant? Almost every time! How many times have I devoted hours to writing a few lines only to mark them out in black Sharpie the next day? This is not a bad thing. For me, the best part of a book is the beginning, before it is even a book, when I'm free of expectations and deadlines. Poems are just poems, and yoga is just yoga. More practice than contest. The privilege and curse of the poet is that the world revolves with or without the villanelle you just can't get right. You can always start over, take what you need and leave the rest. Whatever happens on the page or on the mat, life is enriched by your practice.

landscape/heartbreak: the archeology of a chapbook

~Michelle Peñaloza

My chapbook, *landscape/heartbreak*, came from my idea to discover a city through people's emotional landscapes, people's landscapes of trauma, within the physical landscapes of Seattle. The poems and the other "stuff" of the chapbook (the maps, the essay) grew from the actual walks I took with people to places in Seattle where they'd had their hearts broken.

In the summer of 2012, I lived in Oregon. Post-graduate school, I'd stayed in town to adjunct at the university. I was mired in a toxic and traumatic long-term relationship. I stopped telling my mother and my closest friends about the lies I caught him in, the endless patterns of our fighting, the difficulties I had concentrating or sleeping. For a couple years, I'd been compartmentalizing these traumas; I had a brief respite that summer, however. I was away for extended periods of time at a writer's retreat, a conference, and The Long Walk—a land performance, art experience—a nearly fifty-mile walk from Golden Gardens to Snoqualmie Falls over four days with 50 strangers. Over the course of The Long Walk, an intimacy developed among our group—in conversation and in our collective moving experience. When we have nothing but time and the path before us, the quality of our conversation deepened. The measured answers I might have given, the self-consciousness I might have felt—I walked past that with other people. Through it.

That summer gave me back pieces of myself; it was the beginning of what gave me the strength to leave. The Long Walk, in particular, helped me rediscover a fortitude I had forgotten.

Fast forward to December 2012: I left Oregon, left that relationship, and decided to relocate to Seattle. I found a place to live, but I didn't have a job lined up. It was on my mother's couch, during the holidays, before moving to Seattle, that I came up with the idea that would become *landscape/heartbreak*.

Upon arrival in Seattle, aside from looking for work, how else would I spend my time? I thought about how the act of walking had given me the strength to leave, how those walking conversations had been clarifying and heartening. My own heart, still raw, still hurting—I thought, what if I asked other people to walk with me? What if I learned the landscape of Seattle through people's stories? What if my heart could heal in tandem with others?

The development and execution of *landscape/heartbreak* happened over the course of two years. Upon arrival in Seattle, I applied for and was ultimately rejected for a grant; however, that initial setback helped me define and refine the project's aims, and led me to create my own Indiegogo campaign, which led to the creation of more "texts" related to the project and to more people learning about and volunteering to take part. I applied for more fellowships and grants in Seattle and was fortunate enough to receive support from literary and arts organizations in Seattle. Completing each application helped me to further hone all aspects of the project and each acceptance provided legitimacy, resources, and monetary support for *landscape/heartbreak*. Additionally, as people learned about the project, I was approached by The Henry Art Gallery to have the project be a part of their Summer Field Studies exhibition and by The Short Run Festival to conduct a walking tour/reading of *landscape/heartbreak*. The project continued to evolve and develop through opportunities such as these.

From September 2013 to September 2014, I walked 119.92 miles with 22 people who shared a diverse range of stories—people who'd lost children and mothers and fathers and lovers, who'd been cheated on and lied to, who'd cheated and lied. People whose hearts were broken by false expectations, by the unkindness of others, by systemic and institutional racism and oppression, by the unexpected realities of adulthood.

I had a sense, at the start of the project, that the poetry that would come from *landscape/heartbreak* would ultimately be a chapbook. I was open to the possibility of a full-length collection; however, as I continued on the walks, the necessity of a set timeframe became clear. The amount of heartbreak and the number of people who have stories to share are infinite. If I hadn't decided to limit the walks to happen within the span of one year, I would probably still be walking with people today. I wanted to be realistic about my own capacity and energy; I didn't want to diminish anyone's experience or my own or my writing in response to people's experiences due to my own exhaustion, physical or emotional. I was wary of how the project could become unwieldy, emotionally and creatively, if I took on too much.

The idea that a chapbook is less comprehensive than a full-length collection rings false in my experience. If anything, the knowledge that I would be working with fewer pages made me prioritize and include only the strongest poems in the manuscript.

As far as my process in ordering the chapbook, I thought about creating a way for the reader to experience the accumulation of narrative, emotion, and discovery that I experienced when people took me on walks. Giving context to the project and my own investment in it—where did this idea come from?—seemed key to communicating this accumulation and was the impetus for writing the nonfiction essay in vignettes, "Notes From the Field," which begins the chapbook. I asked myself, "If someone had never heard of the project and just picked up the book—what would they need to know to find the poems meaningful on multiple levels? How could I communicate the breadth of the project?" I also wanted the reader to experience seeing and engaging with Seattle's mapped, physical landscapes and its storied, emotional landscapes. This led to framing *landscape/heartbreak's* text with the two maps—one blank, at the beginning, and one filled with the routes of the project, at the end.

In reference to the order of the poems themselves, I thought about accumulation as well. I wanted to begin with "Pentimento," a poem in couplets, which works in the mode of layering and accrual—a catalog of simultaneous narratives in different times and spaces within the specific place of Seattle and the surrounding area—to allude to the idea that the stories in the landscape and within this collection are, and have always been, here. From there it made sense to move from my own heartbreak into the various kinds of heartbreak—moving back and forth from the specific to the broad—the order interspersed with what might be expected and what might be a surprise.

I wanted to conclude the chapbook with an all-inclusive, composite piece, which became "Field Notes." A great anxiety of mine throughout the making of *landscape/heartbreak* was the task of doing justice and paying homage to the openness and vulnerability of the people who took me on walks. Not every walk inspired an entire poem. Not every attempt to write a poem was successful enough to do justice to a story someone had shared with me. There is a whole pile of attempted stop-starts that did not make the cut, which could make up another chapbook (that should never see the light of day). Yet, I still wanted to acknowledge every walk as a part of the project, as integral to the whole even as some appeared as entire poems, in parts of poems, or only in "Field Notes." This final poem, which I aimed to also correspond with the final map in its form, is comprised of small pieces—vignettes, details and snippets—arranged in the chronological order of each walk. I conceived of these smaller pieces as "inside poems" shared between me and the people with whom I walked. These small moments may read as more esoteric than the rest of the collection, but it's my hope they resonate for every reader, and I believe, taken as a whole, will reiterate the culmination of story and transformation of place in *landscape/heartbreak*.

Developing a Spine: From Chapbook to Full-Length Manuscript

~Kristin Berkey-Abbott

When I was a younger poet, I imagined that my publishing would follow a well-established path: publish a chapbook to begin, and then publish a collection every few years. Poets for centuries before me had followed this route. As the century turned from the twentieth to the twenty-first, I studied the books of my contemporaries looking for clues to put a book-length manuscript together, especially a first book. I noticed how many poets built a first book out of a previous chapbook. It's a time-honored tradition, but it may not always be the best approach.

I have yet to publish my first book with a spine, but I've published three chapbooks. I understand the appeal of building a book around one of them. It takes some of the anxiety out of the process. In the early stages of book assembly, we may wonder if we have enough poems. We may wonder if we can really put together a book-length collection. We could console ourselves with the knowledge that we've already created a chapbook, so a good chunk of work is already done.

Similarly, when I was in graduate school, I felt anxious about my ability to write a dissertation. The best advice I ever got was to think of it as a series of connected course papers. I could write a twenty-page paper, and I often did that in a single weekend. If I thought of the dissertation as 6 or 7 course papers, I felt much less anxiety.

You might have yet to publish or assemble a chapbook, but this process of visualizing the larger work in smaller chunks can help in the early stages of the book creation process. In graduate school, I knew my topic early enough that in fact, I did write a course paper or two that I used to build the dissertation. As we write individual poems, we could also be taking notes about how they'd fit together with other poems we've written, be it a chapbook or a larger work.

Create three chapbooks around a similar theme, and presto: a book with a spine. Most poets don't follow that exact process; I rarely see a larger volume that includes a whole chapbook, much less multiple chapbooks. Still, it's a good way of conceptualizing the larger, book-length manuscript.

When I create a chapbook, I've already chosen a set of poems that revolves around a theme. Even after I've published a chapbook, I often return to the same theme. I'm interested in how time changes the way artists respond to their ongoing interests, and a chapbook can serve as a building block. If one chapbook works as a building block, several might be even better.

But is this approach the best one? A chapbook has been designed to stand by itself. If we take the whole chapbook, or even just a selection of the ten or fifteen best poems in a chapbook, and plunk it into a book with a spine, we have the additional decision of whether or not to make that section stand by itself or to weave the chapbook poems throughout the larger volume. We run the risk of the poems never fitting in with the others if we leave the chapbook section standing by itself. But if we weave the poems throughout a larger manuscript, we may lose some coherence; that loss might be worth it in the service of the larger work. The poet who uses a chapbook to build a larger volume must use extra discernment.

Another danger with this approach is that the book can become repetitious. The editing poet must be rigorous to make sure that one symbol/image/word/phrase doesn't dominate the book that's organized around a theme. That's a task we should never overlook as we're creating larger collections, but if we start with a chapbook as a building block, we might be more likely to be repetitive. Even if we're aware of the danger, we might trip over this obstacle.

Reading the work out loud, poem by poem, page by page, in one sitting, can help us discover repetition in a way that reading silently does not. When I did this with one 72-page manuscript, I was amazed to see and hear how often I repeated the word "cozy"; I had no idea that I used that word more than once until I read my work out loud.

There are other reasons why we might want to include one or more chapbooks as part of a larger collection. My first chapbook has outlived its publisher, and that's not an uncommon fate for a chapbook. If I include those poems in a larger book with a spine, I give them a chance at new life and the possibility of being preserved in new ways. It's the rare library that keeps a vast collection of books that are bound with staples. A book with a spine is much more likely to last a century or two.

As I have assembled and reassembled longer poetry manuscripts that have the potential to be a book with a spine, I flirted with the idea of not including any poems that had ever been in a chapbook. I know that many of my book buyers are likely to be the same from publication to publication. Is it fair to ask those who have bought a chapbook to buy the same work again if I include those poems in a book with a spine? At first, I thought that it wasn't, and I didn't want to abuse the generosity of my audience by including works that had already had their chance in a chapbook.

But some work just begs to be included. Some poems work so well with others that it seems cruel to keep them apart. In the end, I've allowed a compromise. I will use poems from published chapbooks, but I will spread them across the manuscript. And I will try never to include more than half of the poems from any given chapbook. That way, my most faithful readers get the pleasure of seeing old poems while they also have the joy of discovering new ones.

There's another reason to include some poems from past

chapbooks. In an ideal world, the book with a spine will reach new readers who might want to go back to discover those earlier chapbooks. Including the best poems from those chapbooks might entice readers to buy those works too. We might even argue that we have an obligation to our past publishers as we move forward.

In the end, I try to remember what I've always told my students: don't get so bound by rules that the work suffers. The main decision we must make on our journey from chapbook to a book with a spine is what is best for any given piece of work.

Write For One Person Who Is Not You

Interview with Nickole Brown

DtM: In this ever-growing poetry world, with so many poets publishing books, what makes for an outstanding poetry manuscript?

NB: Tough question. I don't think I could answer that definitively other than to say this: *I know it when I see it.* I could say it has something to do with attention to language, to economy and lyricism, but what writer hasn't already heard that in workshop? I could also say it has to do with craft, with an understanding of how a line breaks, of how to pour your poem into the right form, but that too is something that we've all heard before.

I suppose the greater point I'll make then is that the best books I've read take great emotional risk. More accurately, these books eschew the tendency of so many contemporary poems towards obscurity and irony. They trade in that safety and instead say something difficult, plainly, right there in the open. I mean, there's always the chance that poetry of this nature is going to read as sentimental, that someone's going to slap the dirty word "confessional" on a book that takes this road, but the deep kind of truth telling I seek in poems is bigger than that. I'm talking about books of poems that defy prescribed, expected emotion and go straight for the thing that's the most difficult—even impossible—to say. Laure-Anne Bosselaar's "Amen" in her gorgeous collection *The Hour Between Dog and Wolf* does this, as does Brigit Pegeen Kelly's haunting title poem "Song." These are the kind of poems that don't take sides for either villain or victim, the kind of poems that use language without hiding behind it.

That said, I'll also confess I'm terribly attracted to books that maintain their focus on a particular subject or theme. Writers are full of obsessions, and I enjoy entering into books in which a writer has fully surrendered to that one thing they always return to, that one thing they can't quite let go. The stamina required for such a manuscript is difficult to maintain, but provided the topic is deep enough in the poet's blood, it can provide not just a miscellany of observations but a book that truly creates its own singular world. Jack Gilbert's *Great Fires,* while not a "project" book, per say, is a collection that holds together thematically to take the reader into his specific kind of world, but there are many other books that I adore that hold together in even more cohesive, unexpected ways—two of my favorites are Patricia Smith's, *Blood Dazzler* and Maurice Manning's, *A Companion for Owls: Being The Commonplace Book of D. Boone, Lone Hunter, Back Woodsman & c.*

DtM: What trick or technique have you learned in ordering your poetry book that could help someone put their first poetry book together?

NB: I like wide open spaces to spread my poems around on the floor. I like blank walls to tack them up; I like corkboards and clotheslines—any way to physically see the shape that my poems take on the page and then to manipulate the order of those pages, much in the way I might arrange the furniture in a room. This might get a little messy, especially if you have a cat like mine that likes to romp in the pages, but it's well worth bringing the poems out of the digital space of your laptop and into the real world of paper and ink.

When you do this, you should pay attention to the order of the poems, of course, but I'd also advise examining a few other things as well. If you are constructing a collection that braids together various series or sequences, the form a poem takes can help guide the reader with certain visual cues that let them know which series they're entering before they even read the first word. In my second book, *Fanny Says,* for example, prose blocks let the reader know that my grandmother is speaking directly without any intervention from me. A certain stair-step shape indicates lyrical, memory-based poems, and more standard, left-justified shapes are reserved for narrative poems. In this way, the visual presentation of the poem sets the reader's expectation, which hopefully makes for an easier, more fluid read.

Now, in terms of ordering, try, if you can, to think of the through line and the narrative arc you're creating with your poems. You have to read (and re-read!) your poems as if you know nothing of them. First, put them in an order that assists the reader in building a kind of sense of the world constructed by these poems. Even though the order should not necessarily be linear, you should give your reader logistical information as they need it to proceed from one poem to the next. You should also think about the emotional tenor of each piece and how it's going to jostle the mood of your reader as they make their way through your book. Now for those of you old enough to remember how to make the perfect mix-tape, you'll have some experience here—think about your best opener and transition from song to song in a manner that makes an overall compilation that will make the reader want to return to the beginning and experience the collection all over again. If you find that you're too close to your work and can't quite do this on your own, get some help. This is often something that a reader completely new to your work can more easily do.

DtM: If you could give a poet one-sentence of advice in creating their poetry manuscript, what would that advice be?

NB: First, I'll tell you what the fiction writer Harry Crews growled at me once when I was in my early twenties when I asked him the secret to being a successful writer—*Sit your ass in the chair. Repeat.* There's no way around it: writing is work—*real* work in this world—and you have to know that.

Secondly, there's this: *Write for someone other than yourself.* And by "someone" I mean one person, not a whole audience of someones out there who you hope will publish and review your work. Write for one singular person that you want to say something to, that you need to reach. Even better if this person's never read a poem in her life. Maybe your mother. Your sister. Maybe for an artist that's long gone or your cranky neighbor down the street. What I'm saying is that just make sure you're not writing only for yourself. Worse yet, make sure you're not trying to write for the whole of a workshop or for the reading public. Simply pick one person in your mind and speak to them so that they might hear you. You'd be surprised how this one trick can get you out of so many knots of narcissistic navel-gazing or people-pleasing that will flatline your writing.

Yes, that's much more than one sentence, I know. But here's a single sentence: *Sit your ass in the chair— every day—and write until you get through to that one singular person that needs to hear what you have to say. Repeat.*

DtM: What question do you wish we had asked you regarding creating poetry manuscripts? Please ask and answer it.

NB: Is there any advice out there that's really going to make a significant impact in how a poet completes a manuscript?

Of course not, silly. Talk all you want, really, but here's the thing: we learn by doing, by pure, terrifying experience. So get to work. Be brave. Be fierce, even, if that's what's required. Take critiques in workshop and suggestions in craft books for what they are— little Styrofoam lifesavers thrown to you while you thrash around in the water. Everyone who flings one out to you hopefully means well. You can hold onto that lifesaver if you need to, but you can't climb onto the boats from which they come. No. You've got to build your own boat for that. You've got to learn to tread and start building.

Patterns of Obsessions: The Creation of a First Book

~Corrie Williamson

When I first began to attempt an ordering and arranging of poems that would become my first book, I was aware of just one thing that connected them all: *digging*. A dual poetry and anthropology/archaeology major in college, I'd spent my summer after graduation working for the University of Virginia's Archaeology Department—a mostly desk-bound data-entry gig that had me peering bleary-eyed over 100+ year old excavation data of Chaco Canyon and entering the lengths of door jambs, windowsills, vigas and latillas, one by one, room by hundreds of rooms, into an online database for eight hours a day.

What had made the position worth taking (other than the daily sneak-breaks where I hacked poems into my Gmail draft box, prepared at any moment to hit the minimize button) was the five weeks I'd spent at the job's start as part of a tiny survey team actually *doing* the archaeological work in Chaco itself, a remote Pueblo archaeological site in western New Mexico far more humbling and mystical in person than the attic of Brooks Hall where I entered my measurement data.

That summer, sifting through pottery fragments and walking the tops of mesas in the dry heat during the day, and wrapping myself in flannel to watch the sun shatter into a red sea and listen for coyotes at night, haunted me relentlessly. I tried for some time to write about it, gave up, would tinker away, give it up again, despondent. About four years later, in graduate school for my MFA, I finally got the poem out of that experience I'd known was brewing, was coming slowly round to itself. It came like the flooding of slot canyon, pouring out over one Christmas break.

It was a long poem, a series, written in ten parts, and was something of a breakthrough for me. In terms of the manuscript I was amassing, however, and working towards as my first book, it was clunky. It's set in New Mexico, naturally, while the rest of the manuscript was largely bound to my childhood country of rural Virginia. It's eerier and more lyrical than the rest of the book, it's voice at once more surreal and more knowing. But I knew, even in the earliest stages of putting the manuscript together, that it had to go in—that it *belonged*, somehow. The task at hand, then, was to figure out how, and to make it *fit,* to build a book around it.

Archaeology as a revelatory metaphor permeates the poems in my first book, and I recognized this readily enough. But so what? I knew the digging element was present and distinct, and now believed I had an anchor to accompany this central guiding metaphor, but I was at a loss to organize from there, and floundered among various iterations and random compilations. At one point, laying in a pile of my potential pages like a kid in a fall leaf mound, I was struck with a memory of something the poet Charles Wright had said in a workshop that left me dumbfounded at the time, and then wandered out of my memory in the intervening years. He'd told the class, undergrads brimming with a sense of our endless originality and promise, that we all only had a few real topics we'd ever write about, and that we'd spend our creative lives hashing them out over and over. *Huh?*

It had disturbed me enough that I'd written him an email about it, for clarification. He wrote back: "We all have five or six core ideas in our lives that we tend to rework and rework. If we're poets, they come out as poems and their attendant variations. If you're a barber, it's haircuts. Dante, remember, just had one. But it wasn't too bad."

Was I doing that? And, if so, could I spot it, and use the spotting to help me order and arrange what seemed haphazard, jumbled, disjointed? And so I went in search of the patterns of my obsessions.

When I began looking for them, they rose to meet the eye. I already knew I had developed a seemingly macabre little triad of poems that referenced my father and gravedigging. (*What am I going to do with these creeps?* I asked myself routinely as I struggled to find cohesion and shape for the book.) The first of these was about burying a farm animal, an old goat I had grown up with, companionary as a dog. Another was about Dad's pronunciation: "when you said, '*We had to bury the old man / in winter, with the ground frozen,*' the word rhymed with *fury*, not with *tarry*.") The third poem told the story of multiple December deaths in his family, his own father and his brother, and the ground too hard to pierce and dig. I had pinned down this central breaking ground/digging/burying thread, and it ran readily alongside the long archaeology sequence, and other poems about remains, history, etc., that had brewed alongside one another. Suddenly this common note seemed to sing out everywhere, like a silver thread I'd unknowingly stitched into all the poems and was now holding a flame to. I began to see a four-section sequence setting itself up in my mind: the three dad poems, and the long chapter on Chaco, which I called "Ruin Song" (and considered, and rejected, for the book title—but that's another story).

Once I started there, with "Ruin Song" as my anchor, with its themes of burial, unearthing, seeking, and remembrance, and the three central digging poems creating an early symmetry and pattern, I began to look for more. Did I have three of anything else that I could start to build patterns with alongside the dad digging poems?

It turns out I did. I had exactly three persona pieces I hoped could find a place in the book—Xanthus, Achilles' immortal warhorse, stuck in a down-and-out rodeo job in Texas; a whaleman addressing his distant shorebound wife; and a historical piece in the voice of the Comte de Buffon of France, a nasty naturalist to whom Thomas Jefferson had made it his mission to ship a taxidermized moose. (He succeeded, and the

Comte died shortly thereafter.) In a book that's largely consistent in its author-perspective narrative, I had been worried these three didn't have a place.... But what if they operated as part of the pattern? If they created a kind of mirror of one another and the role of stepping outside the central voice to attempt, as "Ruin Song" suggests in closing, "to know the others"?

I was symmetry-hungry, then, and soon realized I had an older poem, but one I hoped to include, called "Portraits of the Anthropologist," written about three kooky and wildly interesting professors I'd had at UVa, a single poem at the time, divided into three sections. I began chopping them up, retitling them "A Study of the Anthropologist I, II, and III," respectively, and spreading them into the three chapters structured around the archaeological anchor. (In the end, I wrote a fourth one of these, titled "A Final Study of the Anthropologist: Self Portrait." It was the only poem I wrote *for* the book, a piece I felt was needed to round out the work and which I fully intended to tie off the loop on my themes. It's the last poem in *Sweet Husk*.)

A book skeleton had unearthed itself: four chapters, three with a quiet symmetry, and one that stood out at odds structurally, but anchored and enforced the book's central concerns—a kind of aberration to draw attention and meaning to the symmetry of the others. From there, I began roughly parsing out poems given their style and topics—not too many animals here, a spreading out of history and other archaeology-informed poems, fronting some of my strongest poems in an effort to win over short-attentioned screeners and readers.

Having recognized my core obsessions and built my pattern around it, I ended up with one quirk to my four sections, which was to kick off the book with a single poem on its own, first and before the sections start. Called "Remains," and written for a girl from my hometown who went missing and whose body was discovered by a farmer on the edge of one his fields over a year later, the poem establishes so much of the patterns and obsessions of the rest of the book. "Anatomists and archaeologists call them / *disarticulated bones*, as if the scattering / of our bodies made us voice less. As if / dead but whole we might still speak," it begins, calling forth the role of anthropology, the acts of burial and exhumation, the desire to listen and learn what we can from what remains.

Once I had identified, and articulated, my own core topics, I could arrange them so that their placement amplified their statement. The patterns give the book structural weight, allowing it to echo and reverberate upon itself. That's not to say I wasn't rearranging it and slipping poems in and out until the last moment. I was solid on the four sections, but I moved the "Ruin Song" chapter into every possible configuration, but where it landed, as the second section, was ultimately right, allowing the pattern to establish itself, be broken briefly by the anchor, then reappear and repeat again to carry the book home.

At UVa, we used to gigglingly refer to Charles Wright as Mr. Right—starstruck as we were by his Tennessee drawl and his poems that took our heads off and that one time he dropped the F-bomb fiercely in a workshop—and in this case, he was. Digging for my topics, for my own central ideas and the patterns they made, I found the lattice on which to arrange the poems.

I still ask myself: how many topics do we really get? Have mine changed? Will they change? I can say that my second book, *The River Where You Forgot My Name*, did not rely on this pattern of obsession and symmetry at all, though admittedly that book emerged more fully formed in my mind as a narrative and historical arc. I'm grateful still for Wright's wisdom, and where it's gotten me, and consider often what it might mean for other creative pursuits. I try to remember it when someone is giving me a haircut.

Mild Peril: A Conversation on Collaboration

~Jessy Randall and Daniel M. Shapiro

Jessy Randall and Daniel M. Shapiro began collaborating on poems in 2003. They are the coauthors of two poetry collections: *Interruptions* and *What If You Were Happy for Just One Second.*

J: What if we wrote up our thoughts on collaborating, in a collaborative way?

D: We could format it like a dialogue.

J: I like it. I'll begin. Do you remember how we got started collaborating? What our mindset was? Did one of us take the lead?

D: My thought process over several years, I guess, was A.) Will we collaborate on more than one poem in our lives? B.) She wants to submit poems to journals. Sounds fine. C.) She wants to compile them into a manuscript and send it out. Sounds fine. This is not to say you wanted to do everything and I was along for the ride. I just remember considering myself a factotum sort of writer (someone who had been writing in various genres as a job), but I considered you a poet forever.

J: Pardon me while I go look up the word *factotum*. Okay, yeah, you had been a reporter, and you'd written catalog copy, but we got to be friends in high school when we were on the literary magazine together (well, actually, even before that, but that's a good enough description), so I've always thought of you as a creative writer.

D: Well, I didn't feel like I had much confidence to move forward as a poet, especially as one collaborating with someone who had been doing it well since elementary school or whenever. In other words, if I hadn't had you, I probably would've thought "meh" and not pushed myself—even though pushing myself was what I actually wanted.

J: We've talked before about how collaborating meant we were more than the sum of our parts (ew, parts?). Neither of us could give up on a particular poem, or the project as a whole, because we'd be letting the other person down. So, as in a marriage (ew, marriage) we took turns being the dragged or dragger.

D: Right. In fact, we could talk about the collaborating aspect— how to choose a collaborator, for example, if you say, "Hey, I want to shake up my writing a bit, and I would love to do that by writing a series of collaborations." I think people might not want to jump in because they're worried about how to edit each other, how to abandon things that don't work, etc.

J: The letting each other down thing also applies to editing. If you think something is bad, you don't want the other person to get blamed for it. You have to be brutal and say, we should cut this. Of course, at first we were too polite to do that and that's why it's good that a book takes literally years to write.

D: We started writing the poems in *Interruptions* in 2003, and the book came out in 2011.

J: We did most of the writing for both books with you in Pittsburgh and me in Colorado, by email. When it was time to put the manuscript together, we got together in person, in Colorado. I remember you came to Colorado and we walked around and around my dining room table discarding and ordering and reordering.

J: Since I'm the self-designated archivist for this, I'm going through the pages right now and remembering a lot more about our process. There were about 120 poems to start with, on sheets we labeled **early, middle, end, early/mid, anywhere**, etc., and also things like **discard?**. One says **only f-word in whole book, cut?** There were a bunch of sheets in a row all labeled **persona** which I guess we decided to keep together in the middle, or at least we did with that draft. We got the total down to about 80 poems.

D: I still struggle with sequencing. It helped me a lot that we wrote the poems together and got to decide the order together. On my own, I'm terrible at that and often kind of give up. When we were doing the writing part, I felt at ease.

J: I'm trying to remember how we thought about the "arc" of our book. Like, why were some poems going to be early, some late?

D: I don't know, but when I arrange poems for readings, I usually position lower-key poems before big production number poems, because the lower-key poems set those up well. Albums are that way: *Thriller* goes from "The Girl Is Mine," which I consider awful, to "Thriller," and it makes the song "Thriller" better. I don't know if I thought about the order of our poems that way.

J: For *Interruptions*, we had a multipart poem called "Animals," and we decided to break it up into individual animals. So we physically cut the print-out of that poem into pieces, with scissors, and then we taped to the pieces to colored construction paper sheets I had at my house. My kids were young then, and many of the construction paper sheets were pulled out of the recycle bin and had drawings on them. So, it's a really crazy-looking manuscript, spread out on the table. The colored pages were the animals poems, and we decided they needed to be spread apart equidistantly.

D: Yes. I remember doing that with the animals. They wouldn't have worked well as a group. Spread out, they're interruptions. Though I always felt the title was a reference to us interrupting each other.

J: The construction paper versions are numbered, and then we put five or six poems in between each of those. All the work we put into ordering the poems now seems kind of silly, because I don't think anyone reads a poetry book from start to finish in one sitting. So, the whole idea of the arc or the structure is basically a crutch.

D: I agree with that about structure, in general. But figuring out an order was definitely helpful for when we did readings.

J: That's right, when we did readings from it, we always did the poems in the same order they were in the book. It was like a cheat for doing a good ten-minute or thirty-minute set.

D: If I were to give advice, I would say not to spend too much time on order.

J: And some editors are going to have opinions about it, so there's no point getting super attached to a particular order.

D: Just look for practical problems or benefits. So if two poems use the word "factotum," don't put the factotum poems next to each other.

J: That's right, we're supposed to be giving practical advice, aren't we? If you only have one poem with the f-word, maybe cut it, or maybe add two more f-word poems sprinkled elsewhere.

D: A friend of mine mentions her deviated septum in a couple of poems, so I tell her not to put those together unless she wants "My Deviated Septum" to be her chapbook.

J: Yes! There were definitely poems that had to be next to each other, and poems that could not be next to each other. Okay, onto finding a publisher. We applied for and received a so-called micro-grant from the Pikes Peak Arts Association, $200 to pay contest submission fees. We also sent the manuscript to Pecan Grove Press, one of the few presses at the time that didn't charge a reading fee. (Pecan Grove no longer exists, sadly.) We did not win any contests, or even come close. After so much nothing happened, we decided to cut the manuscript down again, really ruthlessly. In fact, we ended up cutting almost all of the animal poems that had provided the original structure.

D: Some of the poems felt more ephemeral or inside-jokey than others, and I didn't mind leaving them out. Or perhaps they were too "experimental" (I hate that word in poetry) and felt to me like workshop exercises.

J: After we cut it down to about 60 pages, I remember feeling a sense of relief, like, ahhhh, that's better. Of course, I do love to make things shorter, in general. But it felt like, this is what being a real writer must feel like.

D: And then, since we hadn't heard back from Pecan Grove, we wrote to them and offered to send the shorter version, and Palmer Hall, the editor there, said he'd rejected the long version—but we'd never received the rejection. Oddly, he agreed to read the shorter version, and he accepted it.

J: Yeah, that was really wild. If we'd received the rejection, we would never have been so brazen as to try them again with a shorter version. According to my records, the manuscript was accepted in December 2009 with a planned publication date of late 2010. Actual publication date was August of 2011.

D: For the most part, the editors at Pecan Grove did exactly what we wanted, and that worried me a bit because I had (perhaps masochistically) hoped they would exercise their expertise, i.e., find something important that needed to be fixed. Another editor once sent me a manuscript with red all over it. It made me nervous not to have received that from the Pecan Grove people. But in the end, I don't think they missed anything major.

J: And then Palmer sent us a cover image, sort of apologizing for it and saying he wasn't satisfied with it.

D: And it was horrible.

J: Maybe it's okay to say so, now that the press doesn't exist anymore. Maybe we can even include the image, since the perpetrator of that crime is dead. He was so great as an editor – this was just … a mistake.

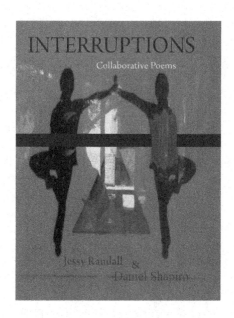

INTERRUPTIONS
Collaborative Poems

Jessy Randall & Daniel Shapiro

D: Is it showing some kind of sun and moon dancing couple?

J: As I recall, we agreed that it looked like a middle school literature textbook with a title like "Horizons" or "Expressions."

D: It made no sense at all for the book. So we suggested a cover with just text, no image, and you sent a mock-up to Palmer.

J: I made that mock-up in a state of panic, like, if I don't get something to them within 12 hours we're going to be stuck with this hideous dancing couple.

D: And he said, "OK. This is great! Let's use this." He didn't change it at all.

J: My guess is that he just sort of threw in the towel at that point.

D: We had a true PG-13 manuscript: one F-bomb and some mild peril.

J: *Mild Peril* would have been a good alternative title.

D: When we started collaborating, and in my own work during that time, I was obsessed with coming up with poems that hadn't been done before or that we could do better. It was nonsensical, but it kept me inspired. I remember when we decided to write our interview poem for *Interruptions* and to deliberately scramble the pieces so questions and answers didn't match up. I figured that would either be ignored completely by publishers, or it would get into a great journal. And it got into a great journal (*Many Mountains Moving*). And that was kind of how I felt about the manuscript. I thought: Who would publish this as a book? Most likely no one.

J: But it sort of didn't matter, to me anyway, because making the poems was such an important part of my daily life, for years. They didn't have to go further than back and forth between us. Of course, then it was awesome when they did go further.

D: A lot of this is rooted in our friendship. I don't think we could write about anything that wouldn't interest both of us roughly equally. Part of the point of collaborating is to take the other person to an unfamiliar place. How would we have stayed friends this long if we had kept doing the same things? I've had friends for, say, a month or two, and we've played racquetball or whatever, and that was the only thing we had in common, so when I decided I didn't feel like playing racquetball anymore, we stopped being friends. I have never wanted to write just racquetball poems with you.

J: Agreed! Also, it was so much easier to be ambitious about the collaborative poems as opposed to solo work, because anything I did for them I was doing for someone besides myself (along with myself). It's way more fun to try to get love and respect for someone other than yourself.

D: The planning and promoting part was especially difficult, and it still is when I'm working on my solo stuff. So I trusted you and knew you had had enough experience sending stuff out, working with editors, etc., that I was happy you took the lead on a lot of that.

J: So that's what collaboration can do—be the insistence from the co-collaborator that this is worth doing. And if the other person believes in it, it must be good, right? It helps assuage imposter syndrome. By the way, thinking about this time in our lives makes my heart feel lighter, because in 2011 and the years leading up to it we had no specter of a Trump presidency looming over us and making us furious and scared every day. If we had done a book now, I bet there would have been a lot more fucks in it.

Do Not Be Afraid

Interview with Jennifer Jean

DtM: In this ever-growing poetry world, with so many poets publishing books, what makes for an outstanding poetry manuscript?

JJ: An outstanding poetry collection has risked falling on its face. It is confident in its vulnerability. Its poems are wholly new and could not have been created by anyone else besides the author of that collection. A fascinating, multi-dimensional personality or voice is tangible in every poem in the best collections. That voice isn't merely "interesting," it is consistently compelling and it satisfies.

DtM: What trick or technique have you learned in ordering your poetry book that could help someone put their first poetry book together?

JJ: If you've written an obviously "themed" or "project" collection, you should consider creating several orderings of your manuscript—each of which follows an intentional strategy. Then hone in on the version that not only assists the reader in understanding and resonating with the theme or topic of your project, but is also the most surprising. Do not choose the version that is expected or obvious. In other words: don't be boring. Be you and be new.

DtM: If you could give a poet a few words of advice in creating their poetry manuscript, what would that advice be?

JJ: Don't force anything—even a "themed" or "project" collection. Editors will know. Readers will know. This is why I'm wary of prompt-driven poems. If the prompt doesn't break down a door in you—if it doesn't even crack a window in you to let in vital, bracing air—then your poems could be merely competent. Your collection could be merely competent—but never fabulous. In other words, make sure the emotional core of every poem in that collection—that the collection itself—is grounded in a tangible part of your soul.

DtM Your first book is about to come into the world! Can you describe the mixture of emotions this book entails for you? Can you describe your journey?

JJ: When my first book came out, I underplayed its significance because I didn't want people to know how happy I was about that miracle. I was afraid of my own joy. I thought people might think, "Who does she think she is?" I let this fear keep me from promoting my book! My advice to debut poets is: do not be afraid. Celebrate! As well, utilize the momentum of your first book to meet the tribe of poets who you can, in turn, celebrate.

With Poems, We Move Towards Book

~Tina Kelley

I write poems, not books of poems. I've never written a poem specifically to fit into a gaping cranny in a book. (Should I have? I don't know!) To write books, I write poems, and then I see how they stick to each other.

In fact, writing a book is a meta version of how I write poems. I collect images, any potentially poem-worthy thought rising day or night, and put them in a file on my laptop. After enough time has passed, I look over these glistening bits and watch for the jolts that jump among them. In geological terms, I see similarities between poetry writing and producing puddingstones—I take some clay (time, mood, willingness to work) and see what pebbles stick to it, what thoughts glom together to grow something new.

I send out the poems I like, fully realizing that 95 percent of them will come back with their tails tucked between their legs. Plus, I'll have to poke a couple of magazines 8 months after submitting, and wait a couple more months of not-hearing-back before considering them lost to the ether. I started sending out poems as a teenager, determined to build up rejection calluses. I've gotten used to rejections, knowing that each poem can't be each editor's favorite.

Over the years, I've learned many valuable lessons about this process, some of which I've actually followed:

1. Read each magazine you're sending to.
2. Only submit to the ones you love. To do otherwise is to apply for membership in a club with disagreeable members.
3. Send regularly to the places that take you.
4. Think of it like applying to colleges, with "safety"

magazines, that can be expected to take a couple once in awhile, and "reach" magazines, where the odds are worse but the payoff more consistent.

5. Build relationships. Be chatty with editors, in person or via letters and emails. Be useful, not just a supplicant at the door. I've even offered to proofread one magazine I appear in pretty regularly—I said I would be reading it cover to cover anyway, and might as well do it when I could catch typos. They took me up on it.

6. When you get a beloved poem published, look back in your records of who rejected it earlier. Think twice about sending good ones to them too often. But first, think, loudly, "neener neener neener!"

7. If you really like a poem, keep sending it out. I think my record is 15 magazines rejecting a poem before a (very good) publication took it. Neener[15].

I usually like my poems a bit better if the world likes them too, and publishes them. I take most of those shiny chosen poems, together with my favorites that I know are good enough even without the outside validation, put them in a big jar, and wait longer for them to ferment, like those brandy-soaked Friendship Fruit Starter concoctions that Amish people make, to put on ice cream, bake into cakes, and share with other Amish people.

Once the fermentation has reached the proper tongue-tingling point, the magpie in me dumps the poems out, checks for shimmer, and sorts them into compatible piles.

For *The Gospel of Galore* and *Precise*, this sorting process occurred while I was blissed out on oxytocin, nursing my daughter, born in 2001, and son, born in 2004. I don't recommend childbirth as a warm-up exercise to manuscript creation, at least not unless you really want a kid as well as a book. But the months after each of my babies was born, I noticed I could sit still for hours, inside, even in gorgeous weather, conditions that usually yank me outside and compel me to bike or hike or explore nature, my inspiration. Lounging on the futon, a baby at my breast, became a perfect time for shuffling poems.

I have a third collection "seeking a publisher," a phrase that irks me, as stacks of paper don't have eyes. Neither do Submittable attachments. I didn't go through the prep of having a baby in order to gestate this third one, *Abloom and Awry*. I did have a pile of poems I needed to put in a pleasing order, and a couple of contests I wanted to enter—after 20 years as a reporter, nothing motivates me like a deadline! And I can see how I've refined my procedure for manuscript-making in the intervening years.

Throughout all three books, my poems have tended to clump into quirky/inviting ones, nature poems, love poems, and ones about procreation. One draft of my newest manuscript actually had the following subheads, which I briefly considered keeping, as they cracked me up: *Ecstasy. Fascination. Love. News. Death. Babies.* It also once had a section of poems wrestling with the universe, right there in the first pages, but that didn't fly with the atheists in my test kitchen—"too Goddy." Like a lead in newspaper articles, my first poems in the collection had to invite, had to take the reader with me, at least through the middle of the book.

I like the sections to be symmetrical, or have pleasing patterns in the numbers of poems per clump. *Gospel* had 15-16-15 = 46, *Precise* was 8-10-10-13-11 = 52, and as it has evolved, *Abloom* has had 9-8-8-9-8 = 42, then 4-10-10-10-4-10=48, and how 1-10-5-10-10-5-10-1=52. Pretty elegant, huh?

It took a long time between my first and second books to be published, but not to be written. They were written about three years apart, but published about 10 years apart. That was the universe's doing, not mine. I spent more time sending *Precise* to contests and big-name presses, and I remember getting positive feedback, but no real nibbles. So I went back to my first publisher, since they are good people who make beautiful books, and they accepted it.

I like to-do lists, especially for large and potentially daunting projects like manuscript making. If there's a problem that could potentially slow my momentum, I'll simply put it on the list and come back to it. It looks something like this:

Put titles in order.
Put poems in order.
Read.

The easier tasks, regarding individual poems ("Do I hate 'Spontaneous Singing'?" and "Maybe the birds should be switched with the starlight? That's deathier..." and "Do I get 'Singing Cure'?") get tackled first, helping me build up steam. I get inordinate pleasure from putting an x on each completed step. The chewier items, like "Figure out why I don't like the first two sections," get procrastinated a bit, but by then, if there are only one or two items left on the list, it's easier to feel almost finished.

Then it's time to send it out to the peanut gallery.

All of us are smarter than one of us, the Internet once said. (The Internet also might have weighed in on whether it's "all of us is" or "all of us are," but I have an essay to write.) Enthusiastic early readers are a gift from above. I have a generous few who will actually read through an entire manuscript and give thoughtful feedback. The best friend a poet could have is a retired English teacher, and I'm blessed with an inordinate number of those in my tribe.

One of them, my dear aunt-in-law Lynn Benediktsson, described for me these great expectations, which I tried to meet. May they prove helpful to others. "When I fan the pages of a poetry collection, I always look for the poems that look different—shorter, longer, with stanzas different, line lengths different," she wrote. "And generally, they are different in kind as well—which keeps me perked up. I usually gravitate to the ones that seem a bit out of the norm to gauge the range. I like surprises and variety, a charge, a provocation to think or enjoy."

Be prepared to notice your poetic tics through this process. Good readers will teach you about them, and isn't it better to be called out by a friend or relative, pre-publication, than by a reviewer, post-? True confession: my best readers recently helped me see that I may be far too intrigued with litany poems. Do my ecstatic lists build in a convincing movement? Should they? Am I a one-note wonder? I went through and found all my list poems, and made sure they weren't huddling together uselessly like seven highway workers watching one guy dig a hole, like reporters at a crime scene, like, um, lists of similes floating limply without a unifying thread.

I enjoy reading the emerging manuscript over and over myself, because that's how I get to know it intimately. I won't know until the third or fourth reading if something consistently delights me, or truly smells bad. If it irritates me slightly on first reading, I'll make a note of it, and see if that continues on further readings. I imagine reading it aloud at a coffee house, and if I can't, out it goes. I try to read the whole thing out loud, start to finish. I try to list the collection's ten best, and ten worst, then write ten new ones that I like better. If a single poem annoys me, even a little, each of the times I read it, I punt it.

All this rereading helps me find repeated images that can smell sloppy, those darlings I've favored so much that they barge into several poems in the same manuscript. And here's a great way to make sure you're not inadvertently talking about the moon or rabbits too frequently: plop the entire manuscript into a word cloud, an online picture that will show you each word in your book, sized according to its frequency. I use wordle.net, and it's always fun to see what the book looks like that way. In *Precise*, my biggest (most common) words were *like, one, God, know,* and *yes.* For Abloom, it's *like, never, know, Simon,* and *one.* (Hmm, someone likes similes!) Just make sure the cloud mirrors your idea of your book.

Here's a habit, short of breastfeeding, that keeps me still long enough to do all this rereading. I've been at it long enough that I can knit while I read, and I love to knit almost as much as I love to write and to read. Knitting keeps me focused, and prevents me from dozing off. After enough practice, it's good for one's poetry, and eventually produces useful holiday presents as well— probably more welcome, alas, in some quadrants of the family, than a beautiful new published volume!

Here's the toughest bit of advice I've gotten, from Gail Martin (author of *The Hourglass Heart* and *Begin Empty-Handed*) via Susan Blackwell Ramsey (author of *A Mind Like This*.) One look at the quality of their work, and you'll listen up: You have to ask this question of your manuscript before hitting send—"Would you be proud of it?"

Poetic Voices: Like Fingerprints
They Are Never Replicated

Interview with Saddiq M. Dzukogi

DtM: In this ever-growing poetry world, with so many poets publishing books, what makes for an outstanding poetry manuscript?

SD: An outstanding poetry manuscript must talk to me in ways that no other collection can. What this means is that the voice might be similar to something I have read before, but it should depict a decorum of language that is uniquely its own. I think about it like fingerprints, every human being has distinct fingerprints that are never replicated, not even by coincidence, in another human being—despite the hands existing from mostly the same design-blueprint, but they are all different, ultimately. That is what I think an outstanding book should try for, to exist in a state of uniqueness. Now this does not mean that each time you write, you must strive to be distinct, remember the fingerprint, they do not struggle to have distinctive pattern, by design they already do.

A poet will not write an amazing book of poems until they have cultivated the confidence to revel in the spectacle that is, speaking in one's original voice. No two people have the same voices, and by extension, I mean story and experience. Even when conditioned to submerge in the same story with other witnesses or participants, the individual perspective of grasping meaning from the event will be completely different and unique, because we have a different way of seeing, a different way of perception, which ultimately enable us to grasp the context and analyze what it means depending on our proficiencies. If we can rely on our unique ways of perception, of course, we bring viewpoints that only us can convey, trusting that instinct in one's poetry is an opportunity to create art that will push boundaries because now there is a novel perspective that is added to the whole field of unfolding voices. For me that is where an outstanding book begins, when it trusts its voice and the narration it brings to the table.

DtM: What trick or technique have you learned in ordering your poetry book that could help someone put their first poetry book together?

SD: This is tricky. Having great poems doesn't make a great book of poems. A great collection boils down to the ordering, how the narration of each poem is like a thread that not only complicates the next poem but enhances the overall narration of the entire book. But I must warn, still, great poems are what make a great book, therefore I encourage poets putting together their first book to concentrate on making individual poems, one at a time, and when they feel like there is a considerable number, they can go through the pile and pay attention to what the poems are saying and how they are interacting with each other.

When I was writing my book *Your Crib, My Qibla,* I didn't think about order, beyond just setting it up as a dialogue between myself, an unspecified voice and my deceased daughter's voice. It was a book long sequence of poems; hence the order was pretty much following the chronology of my grief and the events after losing my daughter.

DtM: If you could give a poet a few words of advice in creating their poetry manuscript, what would that advice be?

SD: Trust your voice and poetic instincts. These will set you apart.

DtM Your first book is about to come into the world! Can you describe the mixture of emotions this book entails for you? Can you describe your journey?

SD: It is hard to talk about the book because it still forces me to relive some of the trauma, I am not ready to confront. Maybe grief is eternal, and it will continue to hurt, but today I don't want to open that door.

Hiring an Outside Editor: One Poet's Experience

~Cindy Veach

It is the rare writer who can view their manuscript with an objective lens. That's the advantage of a manuscript consultation. It brings fresh eyes and new insights that can yield a stronger collection and enhance the chances of publication.

For me, the decision to work with an editor was a positive experience and resulted in just the makeover my manuscript needed. Like most things, however, there are factors to consider before taking this step.

Hiring an outside editor is not free. Cost is a significant consideration for anyone contemplating this avenue. Other factors include identifying the right editor for your work, your willingness to take advice from someone else and engage in the hard work of revision (the editor won't do that for you). In addition, you need to be willing to allow the time and patience required to see the process through.

Because I had come back to poetry later in life (25 years after my MFA) publishing a first collection was especially important to me. I decided to hire an editor after submitting my manuscript to contests and open reading periods for about two years. While the manuscript had received some favorable results (runner up, finalist, semifinalist), it remained unpublished. Throughout this period, I kept revising the collection: changing the title, rearranging, adding, cutting. While I was confident that the overall manuscript was strong, I also felt that something was not right—and that *something* eluded me. Ultimately, the decision to hire a seasoned voice required careful thought and a leap of faith. I was very invested in the manuscript both financially (contest and reading fees) and emotionally. Working with a professional meant not only spending more money in the quest to find a publisher but also entrusting my work to someone else.

As part of my decision-making process, I asked myself whether I could step back enough to hear what an outside person would have to say about a collection I'd labored over for years. Would I be open to taking this person's advice? Was I up for the hard work of revising? If necessary, would I be receptive to re-visioning the manuscript?

I'm a Gemini so, of course, I waffled back and forth before deciding to move forward. The next step was finding an editor I felt I could trust with my baby. I had recently become acquainted with a poet who was a feature at the Massachusetts Poetry Festival. While I had connected with her as a poet at the festival, it wasn't until after the event when I connected with her poetry. Several poems in her latest collection were informed and inspired by history. This was very similar to what I was doing in my manuscript, which uses the history of the textile mills of Lowell, Massachusetts as a backdrop. Because of this connection, I felt confident that she would be able to come to my collection with a unique sensitivity and understanding.

Cost was certainly a factor since I'd already spent two years paying submission fees. At the time, I was very fortunate to be employed and felt that I could afford the investment. The editor I hired did offer a sliding scale pricing model for her services with the fee left up to the writer to determine (within that scale). After the cost consideration, it was important to me to clearly understand the details of what I was purchasing. Typically, editors will offer various levels of editorial input (e.g., organizational input only versus line edits on the individual poems etc.). I opted for a comprehensive review including title suggestions (manuscript and individual poems), line edits, structure/organization, including recommendations on poems to cut.

My editor was a very caring coach. When she had completed her review, she provided the edited manuscript accompanied by a long letter that summarized her recommendations. It began gently by telling me what to expect and kindly warned me that her input would likely be overwhelming: *"My suggestion is to go very slowly because seeing what someone else has suggested about your work can be more than a little overwhelming."* Above all she was clear that the manuscript needed to remain mine. She noted that she was careful to use my words when suggesting retitling suggestions for individual poems and the manuscript. Her input was at all times constructive and productive. I never felt anything but positive energy. Still, the task at hand was daunting and I approached it slowly, reading through everything several times before making a single edit. I then worked diligently through each and every suggestion.

My personal timeline is detailed below; however, every editor's timing will vary and hiring an outside editor does not guarantee publication.

- Editor's review: 1 month
- Revisions: 2 months
- Time from sending out revised manuscript to acceptance: 1 year

Note: the manuscript had to be withdrawn from several competitions/open-reading periods upon acceptance. It may have been offered publication elsewhere but that is an unknown.

Hiring an outside editor is not a solution for everyone. There are many considerations when choosing this avenue and like anything it is important to go into it with eyes wide-open and realistic expectations. Most importantly, there is hard work involved. The manuscript will not revise itself. A writer must be willing to roll up their sleeves and make the hard changes. There are also other options for getting help with a manuscript including exchanging manuscripts with others, asking a trusted friend to review a manuscript, or attending a manuscript workshop.

Several of my poetry peers have decided to hire outside editors. Some have made the decision after submitting a manuscript repeatedly without achieving publication while others simply wanted specific help with one aspect of their collection (e.g. organization, line edits, titling) before beginning to send it out.

For me, hiring an outside editor made all the difference. I had worked on the manuscript for so long that I wasn't able to achieve a holistic perspective. I was in the weeds. My editor enabled me to re-vision the manuscript. The result? A stronger manuscript that still honored and respected my original vision.

II. Behind the Scenes: Thoughts from Editors

I was writing for a number of years but never called myself a writer. That title was for people who lived in Paris and drank absinthe. Then I won a poetry competition and found out the prize was the publication of a debut collection. From one contest-winning single poem to a full-length book! I considered not accepting as I felt the work wasn't ready. Then I saw the date on the letter was the same as the anniversary of my father's death. I took it as a sign. The book, <u>Unearthing your Own</u> went to reprint and the publisher, Bradshaw Books, published my second collection, <u>Toil the Dark Harvest</u> within 3 years.

~Geraldine Mills, *Bone Road in Word and Image*

Infinite Possibilities of Greatness

Interview with Jeff Shotts, Executive Editor and Director of Poetry at Graywolf Press

DtM: In this ever-growing poetry world, with so many poets publishing books, what makes for an outstanding poetry manuscript?

JS: With more poets publishing more books, we have the opportunity to experience more outstanding works.

But I wonder if to answer this question is to limit the infinite possibilities of greatness. Let's not limit the possibilities of greatness. Let's instead agree that we should look up from the page and see more, see stranger, see each other, and not turn away, even from what initially shocks or disturbs us. The great books are those that we are eternally in the state of looking up from. We are thereafter never not reading them. Poets don't will or craft greatness, but strive to add their own infinity to the way we see. I don't want to, nor could I, prescribe what that might look like, but as an editor, I try to recognize works that might forever hold the reader.

DtM: If you could give frank advice to poets submitting to your press, what one sentence would you tell them?

JS: Dare to sound like yourself and no other.

DtM: What is one common faux-pas poets make when they send in their work?

JS: Better to make an uncommon faux pas than a common one. Better to blunder with ambition, bravery, and honesty than conduct yourself or your writing with the scripted language of a resume. Better to sing a new song and help us hear it.

DtM: Who are some of your favorite poets—dead or living? Why do they stand out?

JS: William Blake, Emily Dickinson, Walt Whitman, and Gerard Manley Hopkins, among others, have been examples of those poets, who risked, publicly and privately, a music and vision that are utterly and eternally original. Their works are still capable of snapping us into attention. But this is a list of names to which I would add more names (...Sappho, Langston Hughes, Paul Celan...) and to which I hope to add more names still (the unknown, the unborn, poets writing now who are capable of changing everything). Dead and living, Anonymous is still, across time, cultures, and languages, our greatest poet.

DtM: What is a question you wish we had asked and how would you answer it?

JS: Q. Just who do you think you are?
    A. I'm trying to be Anonymous.

A Lesbian Poet on Running a Lesbian Press and Other Oddments

~Risa Denenberg, Editor, Headmistress Press

That most poetry editors are themselves poets can make for discordant bedfellows. We're always bemoaning not having time for our own writing, lamenting our own rejections, cursing editors who don't bother to notify us yea or nay about our own work, while at the same time promoting the work of other poets. Promoting it with vigor, I would add, because you can't be a poetry editor or publisher without a love of poetry impaled deeply in your flesh.

In 2012, I joined Mary Meriam in her vision of starting a press dedicated to producing books of poetry by lesbians. As far as we knew then, or now, there is no other press with this singular mission. Mary had been publishing the e-zine *Lavender Review* for three years at that point and was particularly attuned to the paucity of places where lesbians could send lesbian-themed poems or manuscripts. *Headmistress Press* produced our first books in 2013 and as of our current list in 2019, we have published 53 chapbooks and full-length books of poetry by lesbian/trans/bisexual women and have published three illustrated books under our new imprint, SallyJane Books. In 2014, Rita Mae Reese joined us, bringing with her the experience of having worked with the lesbian-run Naiad Press in Tallahassee Florida, back in the eighties. Mary designs and produces our books, Rita Mae designs and produces our Lesbian Poet Trading Cards, and I manage our finances, sales, promotional, and distribution activities; we share the editorial work. Amazingly, we live in three widely different regions of the US and have never had an in-person editorial meeting. I like to share our press' story, because with the availability of social media, print-on-demand publishing, and online fundraising, I think it's fair to say anyone who feels passionately about publishing poetry today can do it.

Of course, running an online journal or a small independent press is no easy undertaking. The rewards are found in creating a home for other poets. If you are sending your poems out to the majority of small independent publishers, it's very likely that the editors and staff are unpaid. It's a labor of love.

I'd like for poets to think about that last statement for a minute. While most editors readily understand the emotional rollercoaster of submitting our own work and chalking up rejections, many poets do not similarly think about the editor's position in the dance. For several years, I wrote individual feedback letters to poets who were not accepted for publication in our annual chapbook contest. Although most poets were gracious in accepting the feedback they had requested, a couple of snarky replies were enough to make me wonder if we should offer feedback at all. I don't do it anymore, which is a loss to our submitters. The editorial process is grueling, at times heartbreaking, and every editor reads many more deserving, even brilliant, submissions than they can possibly publish.

In a feedback letter that gushed praise on a splendid manuscript, I asked rhetorically, "So, why didn't you win the prize?" I admit that the process can seem arbitrary from the poet's point of view. My most recent book, *slight faith*, was in circulation for years, being rejected, and later garnering semi- and finalist spots, before it was published. I'm sending my current manuscript mainly to open-reading periods, rather than contests, primarily because there is no guarantee that a contest judge will ever see my poems. There is no certainty that anyone has read beyond a poem or two in the whole manuscript. *Who reads these poems anyway?* the poet always wonders. In the case of Headmistress Press, we do read the manuscripts that are submitted in their entirety and we discuss, debate, and even squabble over the ones we love. Every manuscript is read by at least two editors and the winner and finalists are chosen blindly by an outside judge.

So, as an editor, what am I looking for when I read poems? Things

I love to find are lyricism and word play, surprising leaps of faith, finding the perfect word and not a single word unneeded, fresh language, rich metaphor, and attention to sound. I'm particularly drawn to interiority, emotional honesty, and moments in a poem that make me feel differently about something or question who I am or what I thought I knew to be true. I look for startling endings that turn into unpredictable excursions. At best, I want a poem to change me.

Although everything starts with the quality of the poems, there is much more to consider in putting together a manuscript. When Ellen Bass was asked about her process for composing a manuscript, her answer was, "when I have enough good poems," indicating that for her, there is no great mystery in composing a manuscript. Ellen's a fabulous poet and teacher, but unlike her, most of us struggle tirelessly over that task. However, "enough good poems" is certainly the sine-qua-non criterion. So how do you know if you have "enough good poems?" Or to break it down even more, how do you know whether or not any poem you've written *is* "good?" With a mixture of chagrin and gratitude, I recall how, during a workshop with Dana Levin, she told me, "Your problem is you don't know how to tell your good poems from your bad ones."

Everything changed for me when I realized how much I needed other poets to help me become a better poet. I'm an incurable introvert. As a nurse, I worked in a profession that consumed most of my time and was far outside the world of poets or academia. I rarely attended workshops or went to poetry readings. But moving to the Pacific Northwest brought me into contact with a wonderful literary community. When I joined a writers' group in 2011, it was groundbreaking for me. Unsurprisingly, the growth leap came from reading others' drafts and being compelled to give honest, useful feedback. I've read poetry insatiably since I was a pre-teen. I knew *why* I read poetry but I was never taught *how* to read poetry. Now, I regularly attend poetry workshops, conferences, and festivals; I go on writing retreats; I've developed a cadre of poetry friends with whom I communicate about all things poetry, often on social media sites. Now, I read, write, publish and review poetry. I buy, buy, buy poetry.

So, the first requirement of a manuscript is the goodness of the individual poems. If you are working on publishing single poems or a manuscript, it is well advised to have a mentor, a poet friend, or a workshop group (online, skype, in-person) to guide your understanding of your own skill and footing as a poet. As an editor, I always look through a manuscript for "the best" poem(s), and try to measure if the rest of the poems in the manuscript aspire to that level. It is a far better bet to send fewer poems out rather than sending some great poems along with lesser ones. Once you've set the bar for your manuscript, you have to reach for it with every poem. The process of reading poems with an editorial eye has taught me, painstakingly, to look for elements that divide fully-realized poems from not-done-yet poems. A poem that is not done yet often reads like an interesting sketch or thought waiting for craft to transform it into a poem. Drafts are crafted into poems with specific imagery, heightened language, use of metaphor, and musicality. Obscurity and obfuscation should be avoided, in my opinion. Most readers want to find meaning in the poem; they want some element within the poem to reach towards (at times, even touch) something within themselves.

Conversely, a poem may be well-crafted but doesn't move anywhere, and perhaps needs to ask a provocative question or contradict itself. Another superlative teacher, Ilya Kaminsky, offered this element that also can make or break a poem: *A poem should contain remarkable ideas*. Good poems are interesting; great poems startle, amuse, argue, complain, contradict, and challenge. They show relationships among disparate things through metaphor and images.

I particularly love to pick up a book of poetry and read it front to back because each poem holds the promise of connecting me with the next one—and so on, poem after poem. There are manuscripts in which every poem is perfectly good, some even exceptional, but the manuscript as a whole just isn't working yet. Even with admirable poems, composing a cohesive manuscript is not an easy task. Failures in this area usually have to do with structure, how the poems play off one another, their order, sections, use of quotes and epigraphs, all of which must gel in the arc of the manuscript. In a book with a narrative arc, I like the poems to be presented in an order that builds intensity. This may or may not be a chronological order. Some books order themselves, following a theme, color scheme, story, or set of interrelated ideas. It's a good idea to break it up a little, though, not have all the poems about wild ponies in one section and all the poems about urban cowboys in another. I've heard a great deal about how poets put together their manuscripts; often involving 3 x 5 cards tacked up on walls or pages spread out all over the floor; perhaps it's finding a word at the end of one poem that is mirrored at the beginning of the next poem. As an editor, I appreciate that there are many ways of organizing the work that would make a cohesive book; you only need to find one.

One thing I suggest poets should use sparingly are quotes and epigraphs. I sometimes cringe when I open a manuscript to a page with three or four quotes, usually from favorite poets. (I cringe mostly because I've been guilty of this myself!) Section quotes should point towards the poems in that section or bridge one section to the next. Anytime a quote, phrase, or epigraph is used, it should shove the work to the forefront, otherwise it detracts. And endnotes: please put them at the end, and only if they are really meant to help the reader and not just to show off. If you need to explain your poems, well, what can I say? (I'm sure there are exceptions to this personal preference of mine.)

I've clarified above how I work as an editor. But what am I looking for as a publisher? I need to know that for every several books that we love and publish that only sell a few copies, there is a book here and there with a go-getter author who will be able to promote and sell her book. This is the harsh reality of publishing, we don't get paid, but we do have to stay afloat. And in most cases, if you are submitting to small independent presses, and your book gets chosen (Yay for you!) you need to be prepared for the work of publicizing, promoting and selling your book. You should also be prepared to read well in front of small or large audiences, to be interviewed on the radio, and to respond to other poets who may contact you.

As a summary, here are some thoughts to hold in mind as you move towards putting together and submitting a manuscript:

1. Every poem in a manuscript should be a good poem that has a sound reason for appearing along with every other poem in that manuscript.
2. It's always better to send fewer poems than to stack a manuscript with poems that aren't ready or don't mingle well with others.
3. Find another poet (or poets) whom you trust to read your manuscript and give you feedback on individual poems, as well as on the manuscript as a whole.
4. Be cautious about using too many quotes or epigraphs. If you're not sure the quote enhances rather than overshadows your poetry, don't use it.
5. Look for presses that embrace your sensibility as a poet. Better yet, buy their books.
6. Read submission guidelines and follow them!
7. It never hurts to thank an editor for taking the time to read your work.

What Do Editors Look For, Anyway?

~Kelly Davio, Former Senior Editor, Eyewear Publishing

One of the best—and most difficult—jobs I have as an editor for an independent press is selecting new poetry titles for inclusion in our catalogue. The upsides of the task are obvious: I get the pleasure of discovering new-to-me poets and of offering publication to writers with whom I get to have productive editorial relationships for years to come.

The downsides have to do with the limitations of the 24-hour day; when screening manuscripts, I typically have hundreds of books on my desk (or, mercifully, in my digital submission queue. I don't think my desk could take the weight), all vying for a small number of publication slots. I can't spend hours with each book, much as I might like to, or the collections already moving through the publication process wouldn't get adequate attention.

Instead, like most acquiring editors, I read until I can see that a book either has or doesn't have what I'm looking for before I mark it for a second reading or for rejection.

So just what is it that I'm looking for?

A Good First Impression

Poets know that an opening line must perform an important role in the complete artistic unit of a poem, yet it's easy to forget that the first poem of a collection should function in much the same way; just as a wise writer would never begin a poem with a clunky, out-of-tune line or a toss-away image, a poet shouldn't open a book with a merely okay poem that comes across as purely introductory. That's the literary equivalent of dipping a toe into pool water to see if it might be too chilly.

Instead, I want the first poem of a manuscript to dive—maybe even cannonball—right into the pool's deep end. It should command my attention with a bold move, a gutsy statement, a crackle of humor, a powerful image, smart wordplay, or a moment of technical excellence that not only introduces me to the content of the collection but also lets me know that the poet has come to the page with something important to say and the confidence to say it boldly.

A Sustained Thought

I'd be doing writers a disservice if I gave anyone the idea that front-loading a book with its heaviest-hitting poems is, in itself, a principle of organization. If a book fails to build on the quality of that cannonball-dive of a first poem, I'm likely to feel cheated. Instead, I want to see a sustained thought—an argument, an idea, a story, a belief, a theme—developed from that first poem and articulated throughout the collection.

A question I ask of any manuscript I'm considering is *what is the sustained thought of this book?* In essence, what is the book trying to demonstrate via these voices, images, dramatic situations, titles, and techniques? Is the book, in short, *about* something? Does it have a point? If I'm going to read on, I must be able to find clear evidence of a sustained thought at work.

A second question I ask while vetting a manuscript is *has the poet articulated that thought in an economical way?* Poetry is, of course, in the business of economy: no word should be superfluous, no image gratuitous, no item of punctuation out of place. So too should each poem play an important role in shaping, shading, developing, and furthering the sustained thought of the book; there's no room for purely decorative poems, poems that simply sit mid-collection to fill page count, or poems that—while they may be perfectly good in their own right—don't serve the book as an artistic unit. If I'm going to remain invested in reading the book, it needs to demonstrate focused attention.

An Element of Surprise

Finally, I want a book of poems to give me something that I haven't seen before.

That sounds like a tall order, doesn't it? After all, how is a poet to know what an editor's seen? And given how many poets are writing and submitting work at any given time, is there any topic that hasn't been covered?

Don't despair. I'm not asking for a manuscript about a subject as obscure as Ruth Bader Ginsburg's left pinkie fingernail (though I'm not saying it wouldn't be a worthy topic!). Instead, I'm asking for unique takes and fresh perspectives.

I see a lot of manuscripts about life's "big stuff": family (wanting one, having one, struggling with one, losing one), love (finding it, screwing it up, wondering where it went), art (making it, responding to it, valuing it), violence (enacting it, recovering from it, making sense of it) and death (facing it). There's nothing at all wrong with writing about the "big stuff," but even the most poignant topic grows bland if it's framed in an expected way, or a way that relies too heavily on expected tropes.

What I'm looking for is a fresh approach. I'm not sure I need to read another collection about divorce, for example, but I would be thrilled to read one about divorce as viewed through the lens of theoretical physics. I'm not terribly excited about reading another collection on the desire to have a child, either, but I'd absolutely read one set in a haunted house. It's uniqueness of perspective that has the power to make the old new again, and to excite an editor about your book.

I'd also like to point out that there's a lot of room in the poetry world for collections about "little stuff," too: poems about the secret lives of household appliances, for example, or mile markers along an abandoned highway could make for wonderful collections. You need not feel that you have to write on the same topics as your peers or even your heroes; when you write about what compels you, and about what obsesses your imagination, you seed your book with that all-important element of surprise.

A Diversity of Voices

Interview with Dennis Maloney, Editor/Publisher, White Pine Press

DtM: What do you look for in choosing a manuscript?

DM: We look for poetry that excites, is clear spoken, and holds your interest after more than one reading. With poetry in translation (which is half our list) we try to introduce a wide variety of voices to the English-speaking audience.

DtM: If you could give frank advice to poets submitting to your press, what one sentence would you tell them?

DM: Research the publishers you are submitting to (to see what type of work they publish and if your work fits there), edit your manuscript (or have someone work with you to do it), and craft your poems.

DtM: What is one common faux pas you see poets making when they send you their work?

DM: Many poets fail to organize their manuscript. A manuscript should not be all the poems you have written in the past five years in some random order. There is an importance to organizing the poems within the sections of the book and structuring an overall arc to the collection.

DtM: Who are some of your favorite poets—dead or living? Why do they stand out?

DM: My reading is wide-ranging and eclectic from the ancient Chinese and Japanese of Basho, Ryokan, Han-shan and Tu Fu to the more contemporary European of Tomas Tranströmer, Rolf Jacobsen, and poets I have translated like Pablo Neruda, and Antonio Machado. Among poets from this country Robert Bly, James Wright, and Gary Snyder were among my early mentors. I continually discover voices new to me, among those recently are Ellen Bass, Natasha Tretheway, and Idra Novey. White Pine Press also publishes a wonderful diversity of voices we are quite proud of.

DtM: What is a question you wish we had asked and how would you answer it?

DM: How can poets support the writing community?

DM: I think it is important for poets to go beyond their own writing and support the community of writing in some way. At the basic level this includes reading and hearing the work of their contemporaries; supporting literary publishers (which are largely non-profit) by buying some of their publications; and attending local events.

How to Begin and How to End a Poetry Book: Thoughts from a Judge

~Susan Terris, Freelance Poetry Editor

As a poet, a poetry contest judge, and a long-time freelance poetry book editor, I have a theory about how a poetry book begins and how it ends. Many poets wedge their poems, the "darlings" that have been published, especially if published by significant magazines or journals, into the first few pages of a book. These poets believe that an editor at a publishing firm or the judge of a poetry contest will accept or reject a manuscript on the basis of the first several poems.

There's nothing wrong with this idea if those poems relate to one another and begin to tell the narrative of the book as a whole. Is it an odd idea that a book of poetry, even one without a prominent theme, can have a narrative, tell a story? Well, it is my approach to every book of poetry where I am the writer, the editor, the judge, or the reader. Every book of poetry needs momentum—yes, in many ways not unlike the movement of a novel.

So, this is how I believe a book should start. The first poem, page 1, is always on a recto (right side page). It needs to be short enough to fit on that single page. It needs to be the "way in": a poem that is active, inclusive, invites the reader to be part of the narrative. This first poem needs to be compelling but not so edgy that the reader feels off-put, instead of as if he/she belongs there, feeling the music of the poem and what it promises for the pages ahead.

What should follow that poem? My preference for a second poem is a dynamic and possibly surprising two-page poem that spreads across pages 2 & 3. This poem should have a connection with the first poem but be expansive and contain phrases and tonal clues to what might be ahead. This is the place to be bold. With these two poems, this kind of opening for pages 1 through 3, the reader should feel eager to see what's ahead. And what about those published "darlings"? Put them into a manuscript where they fit. You will need them to add star quality to the book as a whole, not just to its beginning.

Speaking of star quality, some book manuscripts also invite the reader in even sooner than page 1 with a *proem*, a poem that comes before the Table of Contents. Often this is a kind of ars poetica that alerts the reader early to something about the author or to something thematic the author feels is important. In two manuscripts I have edited recently, one now has a proem called "The Flamenco Dancer" and another called "The Lifeboat." Both of these poems are metaphorical. Poet A is not a flamenco dancer and Poet B is not stranded in a rubber dinghy, but both tell something about the imagination and desires of the poet.

For the middle of the book? Not the focus of this essay; but the author's choice of sections and order, should seek momentum, always with the idea that one poem relates to the poem before and after it at least in some tangential way.

But now, let's focus on the ending of a book. Yes, I have a firm idea of what poems should come there. I am interested in the last 3 poems: antepenultimate, penultimate, and last one. For ending a book, an author needs 2 of her/his strongest poems plus a final poem, which is one recto page, lyrical, maybe even possessing a ray of hope, simply a beautiful poem that will connect with the reader and offer some kind of intimacy and ease for the way out.

Writers have a way of believing that the 2-, 3-, or 4-page blockbuster poem belongs as a last poem. I disagree. Many people start by examining the end of a poetry book. Why have the last pages seem difficult and daunting? The antepenultimate poem is the place for daunting and difficult. It needs to be strong and important and even amazing, if possible, and can be more than one page. Caveat: this poem works, as long as the book is structured so that this poem *needs* to be in this place and resists being moved.

Then the penultimate poem is a bridge to the way out. It, too, needs to be a strong, possibly redemptive poem of one page, because it will have the verso (left side poem) position opposite the final poem.

In summary, I am suggesting 2 kinds of poems to open a book and 3 kinds to close it. Is my way the only way? My way or the highway? No, but it is a process, I hope, to make a book manuscript inviting to the editor, the judges, and the reader. Who is the most important of these three? Of course, it's the reader. But with smart and compelling opening and closing pages, a manuscript is more likely to become that book in the hand of eager and awed future readers.

A Subjective Opinion

Interview with Lana Hechtman Ayers, Editor, Concrete Wolf
  & MoonPath Press

DtM: What do you look for in choosing a manuscript?

LA: I look for collections that feel whole, inevitable. I want manuscripts to make me feel deeply, to enlighten me with unique perspectives. I love to be surprised, to encounter beauty up close. I choose manuscripts in which the poems are thematically or sub-textually related to one another, and where each poem informs the next in the sequence in some vital way. Poetry teaches us not only about others and the world around us, but about ourselves. I select poetry manuscripts that allow me to discover something new with each successive reading and make me yearn to keep coming back.

DtM: If you could give frank advice to poets submitting to your press, in one sentence, what would you tell them?

LA: Understand that the editor's engagement with your manuscript will be singular, personal to her own prior experience, informed by a honed aesthetic that may greatly differ from your own as the author of the work, and that this is not a value judgment, but a subjective opinion.

DtM: What is one common faux-pas you see poets making when they send you their work?

LA: All too often poets organize their manuscript according to publication credits, putting their most notably published poems up front. Frankly, I don't even read acknowledgments when choosing manuscripts. It doesn't influence me whether the poems appeared in *Beloit* or were tacked up on the bulletin board at a laundromat. What matters is that the manuscript captivates me from the very first poem and keeps me captivated. Publication credits can't do that. The verse must sell itself with particular language, rhythms, and emotion. I've already given my one sentence of advice to submitters, but here's another: Remember to invite the reader into your work, give them a reason to stay, and level any barriers that stand in the way of open communication.

DtM: Who are some of your favorite poets --- dead or living? Why do they stand out?

LA: Since we're talking about manuscript organization, I'd like to list a few of my all-time favorite poetry collections, books that I return to again and again. Each of these titles stand out because each one provides that complete experience I crave—a collection where the entirety is greater than the sum of its poems, a work that leaves me breathless, glowing.

Lucille Clifton, *Mercy*
H.D., *Tribute to the Angels*
Rita Dove, *American Smooth*
Stephen Dunn, *Between Angels*
Patricia Fargnoli, *Necessary Light*
Alice B. Fogel, *I Love This Dark World*
Carolyn Forché, *The Country Between Us*
Tess Gallagher, *Moon Crossing Bridge*
Joy Harjo, *She Had Some Horses*
Jane Kenyon, *Constance*
Dorianne Laux, *Smoke*
Li-Young Lee, *The City in Which I Love You*
Wesley McNair, *My Brother Running*
Pablo Neruda, *Winter Garden*
Sharon Olds, *Satan Says*
Gregory Orr, *Burning the Empty Nests*
Linda Pastan, *An Early Afterlife*
Octavio Paz, *Piedra De Sol*
Marge Piercy, *My Mother's Body*

Adrienne Rich, *Diving into the Wreck*
Ruth L. Schwartz, *Accordion Breathing and Dancing*

Please note this is a severely abbreviated list, and if I were not being impartial, I would have included all of the authors whose books I've published.

DtM: What is a question you wish we had asked and how would you answer it?

LA: What are poetry book editors thinking?

LA: We editors do what we do for the love of poetry. We fall madly for manuscripts that startle us, that sing to us, that singe us with truth. We admire and celebrate fine works, and we want to share them with the world. Our utmost desire is that poets be happy with their published books. Therefore, we are dedicated to presenting collections in their best possible light.

Most of us editors happen to be poets ourselves, and being poets, we understand all too well the challenges of getting published. Being a poet in a country that values beauty magazines over beautiful verse can be daunting, if not debilitating. As editors, we're here to proclaim, over and over, that poetry matters, and that books makes a difference in all our lives.

We believe no one knows what is best for the poet's work than the poet herself. But if we offer suggestions, we hope poets are open to hearing them. A fresh perspective might allow work to take off in surprising directions. If an editor makes a suggestion the poet disagrees with, a polite refusal is best, free from condescension. We endeavor to treat one another with the respect of esteemed colleagues.

Editors wish to create harmonious collaborations with the poets we publish. We are determined that our authors and their works flourish. We are committed to the marriage of the word to the bound page, or to the boundless e-page. This is our credo: We believe in poets and in poetry, and we faithfully pledge to bring limitless, necessary, powerful poetry books into being.

Trust What the Mind Returns

Interview with Michael Schmeltzer, Editor, Floating Bridge Press

DtM: *In this ever-growing poetry world, with so many poets publishing books, what makes for an outstanding poetry manuscript?*

MS: Most manuscripts I consider outstanding rely on an honest and vulnerable understanding of the poet behind it. They are not ones I could write, not ones that are completely similar to my views or experiences, but ones that some way or another welcome me, let me know I am not alone.

DtM: *What trick or technique have you learned in ordering your poetry book that could help someone put their first poetry book together?*

MS: The first thing I try to remember, even before thinking of a manuscript or its order, is that a poetry book is only as strong as its weakest poem, which is only as strong as its weakest line. In order not to be overwhelmed I take it one step, one line at a time. Eventually, after enough poems have gathered, a passion will present itself. I do my best to trust what my mind returns to time and again (whether it's a single image or idea.)

When it comes to ordering a book around that passion, I think the key is storytelling. Although I consider myself a lyric poet, I think of ordering as narrative. What story do I want to tell with the poems I have? Is it a story from darkness to light, fire to ash, drought to rain? Is it age to youth and back? Again, trust what the mind returns to and tell the story you want to tell, in the way you want to tell it.

DtM: *If you could give a poet one-sentence of advice in creating*

their poetry manuscript, what would that advice be?

MS: Don't be afraid.

As Many Good Techniques as There are Books of Poetry

Interview with Kirun Kapur, Editor, *Beloit Poetry Journal*

DtM: In this ever-growing poetry world, with so many poets publishing books, what makes for an outstanding poetry manuscript?

KK: Naturally, every press, judge and editor has a slightly different sense of what is "outstanding," but when the poet's voice and vision become vivid and palpable, the poetry stays with the reader and the manuscript stands out. Cut out anything that isn't contributing to your singular voice and vision—even if it's a good poem or has been previously published in a good place. The right title helps, too. Editors have to contend with large numbers of manuscripts. A smart, inventive title can help a poem or manuscript become memorable. Use your titles to help clarify the structure of your book or to create cohesion among your poems.

DtM: What trick or technique have you learned in ordering your poetry book that could help someone put their first poetry book together?

KK: There are probably as many good techniques as there are good books of poetry, but here are some that helped me: Divide your poems into at least three piles. You can do this by subject or form or mood or time period—whatever way the groupings seem natural to you. Now, play around a bit. Try to discover as many different groupings as possible. Doing this helps you see all the forces at work in the poems you are assembling—formal, thematic, emotional etc. You may have been focused on the fact that you were writing poems about, say, running away with the circus, but as you shift the poems into piles, you may see that you have sonnets and prose poems, as well as poems about youth and age. Or perhaps you have all lyrics, but some are memories and others present tense, while others are persona poems. To reveal all the possible organizing principles for your manuscript, keep asking yourself, *In what other ways could the poems be grouped?* Eventually, a few groups will seem most important, natural and interesting. These groups may suggest a basic structure for the book or may help you to uncover subtler shifts and movements beneath your larger framework.

Once you have thought about all the different forces at work in your poems, pick one poem that feels like the center of the book. Often, this is instinctual—you'll know where the heart of the book is. Often, it's a poem that incorporates all or many of the themes/groups.

Then, pick a beginning and ending poem that talk to each other in some way. They could be from the same group or a different group, but pick poems that create tension and suggest movement.

Another trick I found useful was to weave poems from each group across the whole structure, so that you create variety as well as echoes of the themes, forms, moods etc.

Keep playing. Keep moving things around. When you find the right structure for the book, all of the poems suddenly come into sharper focus.

DtM: If you could give a poet one-sentence of advice in creating their poetry manuscript, what would that advice be?

KK: Don't give up; revise it one more time.

Thinking Like an Editor: How to Order Your Poetry Manuscript

~April Ossmann, former Executive Director at Alice James Books

In my experience as a book editor, the biggest mystery to emerging and sometimes even established poets is how to effectively order a poetry manuscript. As a poet working on revising and re-revising my graduate thesis toward book publication, I didn't have much idea either. Here's why: Ordering a manuscript requires a different kind of thinking than line editing or revising your poems—a kind of thinking I hadn't been taught. A poet I work with calls it "the helicopter view," which I love. I think of ordering as a kind of three-dimensional thinking, as opposed to the two-dimensional thinking (like using tweezers under a microscope) necessary for line editing poems. Ordering requires seeing each poem from a distance, so that all its sides are visible; it also requires seeing the manuscript as a whole, so that you can decide how each poem and its parts might connect with others in a series.

If the poem doesn't fit the criteria, save it for a future manuscript, for rereading, for framing as a broadside and hanging on the living room wall—but don't leave it in the manuscript. Strength, not length, makes a good book.

It wasn't until the beginning of my tenure as executive director of Alice James Books, in 2000, that I really learned how to order poetry manuscripts. I challenged myself to suggest an ordering strategy particular to the poetic style, themes, subjects, obsessions, strengths, and weaknesses of each book I edited. Excited as I was to be entrusted with the task, I was profoundly anxious. Since I hadn't yet published my first book, all the poets I edited had accomplished something that was still a goal of mine. At the very least they had had their first book accepted, and many had published multiple books. But performance anxiety was a good teaching tool; I was determined to give my best to those poets, and to make sure my best got better. The method I developed is the one I still use, ninety-plus edited books later.

The first thing I do when I edit a manuscript is to consider the inclusion and exclusion of poems, which is a critical part of ordering. It's also perhaps the most difficult editing we perform, because it can mean letting go of emotional attachments. As poets we keep poems in our manuscripts for all kinds of reasons, but there are two inseparable criteria that should govern: The poem is "book strong" and fits the major or minor themes and subjects, helping to create a cohesive whole. We keep poems that don't fit those criteria for several reasons. Sometimes we're attached to a poem because it represents an important emotional moment, phase, or event. Other times we're attached because it's the title poem and "must" stay, even if the wise voice we so often ignore whispers that it's not up to snuff. And still other times we're attached to a poem because we think it's critical to the collection's narrative, themes, or chronology; it was published in a magazine; it's our mother's favorite; and so on.

If the poem doesn't fit the criteria, save it for a future manuscript, for rereading, for framing as a broadside and hanging on the living room wall—but don't leave it in the manuscript. Strength, not length, makes a good book.

Unless the manuscript is overlong, I ask authors for extra poems to consider with the manuscript, and I recommend that poets who are acting as their own editors do the same. Try considering strong poems that may be newer and may not feel as if they belong in the manuscript. I read the manuscript and extra poems, giving each poem a grade: check-plus, check, or check-minus. Then I set the check-minuses aside. If there are enough check-pluses to create a book-length manuscript, I set aside the checks, too, after deciding whether they can be edited up to check-pluses, giving special consideration to those that are thematically important or have great potential but are simply in an early, rough stage.

Then I reread the poems, listing each one's themes and subjects, as well as noting repeated words or images. We all repeat ourselves, but some of us do so more obsessively than others, and that can be a strength or a weakness—or both. Next, I separate the poems into piles based on theme or subject, count the number of pages in each pile and note how many of the strongest poems landed in each, and use that information as one of multiple guides to a successful ordering strategy. I'm not a believer in the one perfect way to order a given poetry manuscript. I believe that the many ways to order a manuscript are limited only by imagination, so feel free to invent strategies beyond those I suggest. It's important to try different strategies and to make a decision based on both intellect and intuition. Go with the order that feels right.

Working with Adrian Matejka to edit his first book, *The Devil's Garden* (Alice James Books, 2003), produced an ordering that felt right to me. As I recall, the manuscript arrived with a roughly narrative or chronological ordering. The collection contains multiple subjects and themes, but in reading the manuscript I noticed a common thread: identity. The final ordering highlights it, delineating how music/musicians, history, art, pop culture, ethnic background, family, and experience formed the speaker's identity. Poems on those subjects are interwoven throughout and ordered to create a sense of growth or evolution (not chronology—the poems jump forward and flash back in time, reflecting how the mind experiences identity), resulting in a thematically cohesive collection.

Ordering strategies I've used include creating a narrative line or arc (regardless of whether the poetry is narrative) and grouping or interweaving themes to create a sense of evolution or growth, proceeding toward a conclusion—not resolution. Another strategy is a lyric ordering, in which each poem is linked to the previous one, repeating a word, image, subject, or theme. This sometimes provides a continuation, sometimes a contrast or argument. Other times I follow one or several emotionally charged poems with one that provides comic or other relief; sometimes I work to vary (or interweave) the poetic styles, individual poem length, pace, tone, or emotion. Some orders build toward a narrative, emotional, or evolutionary climax or conclusion (a "Western ending") and some end deliberately unresolved or ambiguous (an "Eastern ending"). Different poetic styles can benefit from different ordering considerations. A manuscript composed of poems that function in a deliberately nonnarrative fashion might best be ordered according to a strategy of collage, surprise, or juxtaposition—or by creating a faux narrative arc.

Other ordering considerations include whether to heighten or downplay the poet's repetition of particular imagery, words, or subjects. If there are too many repetitions of a word or image, I generally recommend making some substitutions, and placing those poems at strategic intervals in the manuscript. This can create a subtle sense of obsession rather than a numbing one. I also alternate strong and less strong poems, and try to avoid having too many poems in a row on the same subject or theme, except where they indicate growth, contrast, or argument. I may order to heighten the importance and relevance of the manuscript's title or leitmotif, or to create a greater sense of thematic unity. Generally, my suggested order juggles most of these concerns at once, which is where that clear three-dimensional or helicopter view is most critical.

To achieve an order that maximizes strengths and minimizes weaknesses, it's crucial to gain the editorial distance necessary to self-evaluate, to think like an editor. An exercise for achieving this is listing a minimum of two strengths and weaknesses per poem, as if preparing criticism for poetry workshop fellows. Some things to assess are syntax, diction, and voice; either too much or not enough description; the balance of abstract to concrete imagery or symbolism; the flow or rhythm; the presence or lack of tension or risk (narrative, dramatic, linguistic, formal, emotional); the capacity to surprise; line breaks; word choice (the best, most accurate, evocative choice for context); point of view; and the use (or misuse) of dialogue. Noting as many strengths and weaknesses as possible allows for the most objective evaluation of which poems are strongest and why.

I also consider whether a manuscript needs sections and whether the sections will benefit from titles. The current convention tends largely toward creating untitled sections, and that works for many, but isn't right for all. Some progressions are best not interrupted, and some collections don't require the extra breathing space. Valerie Martínez's *Each and Her* (University of Arizona Press, 2010) is a perfect example of both. The poems, ordered as a numbered series without sections, are exceptionally spare and employ metaphor, collage, lists, found poems, fragments, and juxtaposition, all revolving around an emotionally charged subject—the murdered women of Juárez—to create a fractured, incomplete narrative and a tense, riveting progression.

For manuscripts that benefit from sections, I begin and end each one with strong poems that create links between sections. It's important to begin and end the manuscript with two of the strongest poems, but I also recommend giving consideration to which subjects, themes, or poetic styles best introduce the poet's work and the speaker's character within the context of the manuscript, and what the poet considers to be the crucial "takeaway" for the reader. Which lines does the poet want to ring in the reader's ears on closing the book—which are most worthy and memorable?

I don't often recommend titling sections, because it often feels too "telling," too directive, and too limiting of potential interpretations, especially for poetry that employs accessible styles. Titling sections for such manuscripts works best when it heightens ambiguities or adds to potential interpretations, rather than explaining. Titling sections for more elliptical poetry styles can be a boon for the reader, offering an assist without spoiling the mystery.

Other ordering conventions include the use of prologue ("proem") or epilogue poems, epigraphs, and notes, all of which can add to or detract from a manuscript's strengths. As a reader, my expectation for a prologue is that it be one of the strongest and most representative poems in the collection, yet poets often choose a weak one, placing it in the most visible spot in the manuscript. Title poems create a similarly oft-disappointed expectation. In such cases I recommend that the poet omit or line edit and re-title the poem, but keep the original title as the book title. Epilogue poems rarely seem necessary to me but can be a fine or fun choice where they function as true epilogues, offering a bit of the after-story, or in cases where their use is humorous. Even then there's a risk of the epilogue's feeling overly intentional, coy, clever—or just plain unnecessary.

Epigraphs have been such a popular convention for so long that many poets seem to feel they're required for a book to be taken seriously. As both rebel and reformer, I take issue with real or imagined strictures, but some poets and readers simply love epigraphs. Unless I'm editing a manuscript, I tend not to attach much importance to them. For me, they work best where they highlight, comment on, or expand on a theme, subject, or obsession in the manuscript, but if the poet has done good work, an epigraph shouldn't be necessary (poem epigraphs that are noticeably better written or more interesting than the poem should be omitted). For me, they're candied violets on the frosting on the cake, and I happen to like cake best. I wouldn't, however, deny others their candy or frosting.

The use of endnotes is probably the most contentious consideration (some readers find them necessary, some vehemently oppose them). The tradition is that poetry shouldn't need notes, that it should be complete in itself and shouldn't need explaining, but there are many poets and readers who enjoy them, and the types of endnotes employed are multiplying. Notes were once mostly limited to translating foreign words, defining obscure ones, and acknowledging textual appropriations. Now they include dedications to family, friends, or writers; direction to source material or additional sources for further study; and acknowledgment of inspirational sources. As a reader, I prefer few or no notes. As an editor, I'm more flexible, but recommend keeping them as brief as possible. Pages of endnotes can be off-putting, and author web sites or blogs provide a better venue for fun and interesting but extraneous material and notes.

Once I've ordered a manuscript, I let it steep overnight and read it again the next day to see if the ordering still seems good. I recommend this to authors, but on a more elastic timeline: Try going back to read the manuscript at odd moments over a period of days or weeks. Try printing several versions employing different orderings, and then use your intuition to decide which one is best.

III. Moving Towards Publication
Once the Manuscript is Complete

The single most important thing I did to my first manuscript was to identify a unifying theme and to rewrite poems I already had using "glue words" based on the theme and to write about 15 new poems with a focus on that theme that I could distribute throughout the manuscript. There is a strong bias among publishers toward "tight" narrative arcs right now, "projects" and so forth.

~ Linda Dove, *O Dear Deer*

Determining Your Goals for Publication

~Kelli Russell Agodon

Once you've finished putting together your manuscript and feel it is ready to be sent out into the world, there are a few things you need to check in with yourself about before you begin submitting your work for publication. The first question is: *What do you want from this book?*

This may seem like a huge and slightly vague question (it is), but knowing what you want from your book will help steer you away from mistakes and what you don't want. Many poets become so eager about publishing a book that they send it out to any press, even presses that don't have their same aesthetic or presses that aren't really a "fit" for their needs.

This is why it is also essential to ask yourself, *What am I looking for from a press*? It might be helpful to answer the following questions below before you begin submitting your manuscript. Feel free to answer these as journal questions if it helps you collect your thoughts:

What is your dream press? If you could be with any press, who would you be with and why? Are you looking for a press with prestige and status? Are you wanting to be part of a press where you know and respect the editors? Do you want a small indie press where you work closely with one or two editors and may have more control of your book, cover, etc.? Do you want a larger press that may have a budget for more promotion? Are you looking for a press that has good distribution of their books? A local press or something international? Or do you just want to get a book out into the world and really do not care where it lands?

There are no wrong answers to any of these questions; the point is to clarify for yourself what you want.

These questions are important to consider because there are so many ways to get a book out into the world. Knowing what you want will better help you get a plan together. For example, if you want to be with your dream press or a top-tier press, it may take longer for that to happen as presses with more clout may be more competitive due to higher submission levels. However, it's not impossible to have your book accepted by a well-known press, but it may take persistence, perseverance, as well as a very strong manuscript of poems.

There is a wonderful story about a poet who was looking to publish his first book and was determined to get his book into a top press and win a major award. He began sending out his book each year only to the best prizes. While he was doing that, his other friends were getting book contracts (not winning major prizes but getting their books out into the world with micro, small, or mid-level presses). For years, their books came out while he received rejection after rejection. However, he was committed to his goal—he wanted to win a major prize and kept faith in his book. Eight years later, he won the Yale Younger Poets Prize.

If your goal is to have your book placed with a more prestigious or well-known press, you may need patience and determination. You must have faith in your work as well as a strong, well-written, and organized manuscript.

Ask yourself, *Do I want to be with a top-tier press, or do I just want to publish a book?*

If you want to be with a top-tier press, here are some follow-up questions:

1. If I do want to be in a top-tier press, am I willing to wait it out?
2. Have I revised and edited my manuscript so it's the quality my top-tier press is looking for?
3. Is my work even a fit for my top-tier press? (Perhaps, you

write about urban environments and cities, but your dream press only publishes books about nature.)

4. Is there a time limit I want to give myself before I start looking for other presses to publish my book (maybe try for your best dream presses for 2-5 years, then add in other presses you feel would also be a good fit for your book)?

If you just want to publish a book, here are some follow-up questions:

1. What are less "competitive" or smaller presses that might be a good fit for my book? (Make a list and research these presses.)
2. What are the top three things I want from a press? (Answers might be: to choose the cover art for my book, to have more editorial control, to support a local or smaller indie press, to have an exquisite handcrafted or letterpress book, to be with a press I know has good, kind people running it, to be with a press that creates gorgeous covers, etc.)
3. Will I be disappointed if this press doesn't have the budget or social media presence to promote my book?
4. Am I just anxious to publish my book, but will I ultimately be unhappy because I didn't hold out for a better press?
5. Should I self-publish?

Choosing a press is a very personal choice and there is no one right answer. It may be beneficial for you to also recognize that no matter *which* publisher you publish with, your press may not live up to your expectations. While presses do their best, no press is perfect and may not do everything the way you wish, and/or you may not have complete control over a component that is important to you. Maybe you've landed a deal with your dream press, but maybe they are actively suggesting major edits and revisions, which makes you both uncomfortable and insecure. Or maybe you were accepted by the small indie press you wanted, but you're disappointed they can't promote your book the way you would like, or they may not have the budget to enter your title in prizes for published books.

Each press will have strengths and weaknesses, and it's your job as a poet to research your favorite presses and do your best to determine if they are a good fit for you. Think about your favorite poetry collections. Perhaps take all your poetry books down from your shelves or go to the library or favorite bookstore with a large poetry selection and look them over. Look at the covers and the font. Look at the year the book was printed (older books may not reflect what a press is doing now). Which books are you most drawn to? Create a list of presses you feel a connection with, and those you feel would be a good match for your book.

Publishing Today and Working with a Press

Publishing has changed a lot over the last ten years due to technology. So as you are deciding where to send your work, the goal is to know what matters most to you regarding the publication of your book and what your priorities are.

As you begin to send out your manuscript, determine your goals and make a timeline for yourself. For the presses you know you want to submit to, consider buying a few of their books to study the appearance and characteristics of their print books. Do you like the quality of their books? The paper thickness? The font? The cover design? If you see a press only publish books that are a particular size, such as 6"x9," recognize that they may have a standard template they work with and your manuscript will have to fit into that model. Alternatively, if you notice their book covers all have a particular aesthetic, it's important to consider if you'd be happy with a book cover created by this press. You want to be happy with the final product, so this research can be useful so you don't waste your money or time with presses that are not a fit for you and your work.

Distribution:

If distribution is important to you, you may want to research how presses distribute their books and what distributor(s) they use, if any. Some book distributors you may want to look into are Consortium and SPD (Small Press Distribution), two of the most popular distributors for publishers. To find out if a press uses either of these distributors, Google "presses that use Consortium" or "presses that use SPD." Both Consortium and SPD list the presses they work with on their websites. If you have any questions about a press, work to find this information on your own without writing to the press and asking the editors. Because of the internet, most information about presses, their authors, their distributors, and other information are online, which makes it easy to do the research yourself.

Collaboration:

One helpful piece of information to remember is that book publishing is a collaboration between press and poet. It's give-and-take. When you do get your book accepted for publication, it's not wise to arrive with the attitude that you are running the show because you are not. You are working with a press; their job is not catering to your every need and want. They are a press, not short-order cooks. Each press has its own specific and unique way of doing things. Their book covers may have a certain aesthetic (and hopefully, you've researched this and are aware of it), and as one of their authors, you do your best to work within their guidelines.

But recognize, your press wants the best for your book. It's in their best interest to have a beautiful book out in the world without errors and the best quality it can be. They have a vested interest in you and your book. A press is a professional organization, so while sometimes it may feel disappointing that they didn't choose your cover art suggestion which incorporated a cat wearing a space helmet, in the long run, it may be for the best.

Tips to Turn Your Manuscript into a Book:

Once you have done your research and now have a list of presses you'd like to submit to, you need to determine which of these presses have book contests, open submissions, or take queries. There are a few ways to go about this. The most accurate is to look up each press's website and read their "Submission Guidelines." This will tell you if they are taking manuscripts (or not) and when. It will also allow you to become more familiar with their writers and the press's aesthetic.

Other resources to help you find this information would be *Poets and Writers* (a magazine that lists deadlines for poetry book prizes), Submittable (an online platform used by many presses for open submissions as well as chapbook and full-length book prizes), Duotrope (a for-pay platform to keep track of your submissions but also find out who is accepting new work), New Pages (a website to help you learn more about literary journals and publishers), and of course, subscribing to the newsletters of *your* favorite presses to get their up-to-date info of when they are accepting new work.

But whatever each press asks for, follow their guidelines. If they say, "Please don't send a query," don't send a query saying, "I know you don't take queries, but I think you'd be excited about the book I'm writing." As a poet, you want to show yourself as professional and respectful.

Love 'em or Leave 'em (Poetry Book Contests):

One of the most common ways presses find their authors is through running poetry book contests. Many poets have a love/hate relationship with contests; some get bothered by having to pay an entry fee, but many poets have found their way to publication via this route.

One poet said he was no longer submitting to any more poetry contests because "it's just a lottery." He said this because he was annoyed that his manuscript hadn't been chosen yet. A *lottery* is defined as "any scheme for the distribution of prizes by chance." While his frustration is valid, one can disagree with his opinion regarding the use of the word "lottery."

While winning a poetry book contest often includes luck and timing, poetry contests are not lotteries because you can increase your odds of winning in various ways.

When someone buys a lottery ticket at the store, they will not have better odds of winning because they:

1) Combed their hair that morning.
2) Smiled at the cashier and used manners.
3) Paid with a crisp dollar bill instead of one of those faded ones.
4) Pronounced the word "lottery ticket" correctly and use interesting words to ask to purchase one.

When you submit to a poetry contest, you can have better results or have your manuscript chosen as a winner or finalist because:

1) You wrote great poems.
2) You put special care into the manuscript; the poems are well-crafted, and free of errors.
3) You followed the guidelines for the contest.
4) The order of your manuscript is interesting and makes sense.
5) Your manuscript has cohesion, and the manuscript overall has a sense of purpose to it.
6) You chose a strong title.
7) You wrote great poems.

Manuscripts do better in poetry contests if you are a strong writer and have put considerable effort into creating the best manuscript you can. Poetry contests can give your book an extra boost at publication as it's already coming into the world of new books as a "prize winner." Many of the presses who run contests will send the winning book to some or all of the poets who submitted your work, so your poems are already in the hands of new readers. Often these prize-winning books will be featured in magazines such as *Poets and Writers*. Local papers sometimes feature you when they learn their town has a new award-winning poet.

There can also be a lot of buzz around these prizes, especially the larger ones, such as the National Poetry Series or the Yale Series of Younger Poets Prize. Also, many presses have release readings set up for their winners. Plus, it can be thrilling to win—to tell your friends and family that you won a book prize.

But there are some cons to poetry book contests—some are highly competitive with 500-1000 entries (these tend to be the prestigious prizes or long-running prizes), and most reputable presses understandably charge a reading fee. These costs can add up, and if you are finding yourself short on cash, this may not be the best route for you financially.

Some poets "reframe" their submission fee as a donation to the press, but with the chance to be published, possibly receive feedback, and build a relationship with the editors and readers. Others choose not to enter contests that charge a fee. As a poet, you get to decide what is best for you. While many presses wish they could do away with submission fees, publishing and promoting a book can be expensive as well as running a press. Unfortunately, poetry book sales aren't often enough to keep a press afloat financially. Also, a press may be trying to pay their editors and readers, and reading manuscripts can be quite time-consuming. Presses often hire a judge, whom they pay for choosing a book. There's the cost of book production, promotion, author copies, review copies, and other expenses, such as overhead costs (rent, electricity, Wi-Fi, etc.), plus paying their staff and editors. Some poets may be under the illusion that presses are getting rich with these contests, but in many cases, these contests are allowing presses to continue to publish new books.

In modern-day terms, the cost of a contest submission might be roughly equivalent to a visit to a museum or buying a new book. Ask yourself, *how much can I realistically spend on submission fees?* Again, there are no wrong answers here. If possible, keep a separate checking account dedicated to your poetry expenses. You may also determine that instead of an expensive dinner out, you'd rather allocate that money for submission fees or other expenses when putting together a book. However, if you genuinely are under financial hardship, do write to the press to ask if the fee can be waived or if you can enter under a discount. Some presses have recently started to include discounts for BIPOC poets, people living with a disability, students, people on a limited budget, or anyone under financial hardship. Check each press's guidelines to see what they offer, and again, if there is a particular press you wish to be at and truly can't afford the submission fee, do write to them to see if it can be waived or discounted.

That said, if you don't want to submit to poetry presses that charge a fee, there are other avenues to consider.

Open Submissions:

Open submissions are precisely what they sound like—when a press opens its doors for submissions (either through Submittable, email, or snail-mail). Sometimes these open submissions may be looking for a specific type of manuscript or poets, such as they may be looking for hybrid poetry manuscripts, or they may only be open to poets of certain regions or ones who have (or have not) previously published a book. Some presses will have an open submission call, but they are only for a selected number of manuscripts, so be warned—these open submission calls can be closed by the time you wake up if you're on the other side of the country. For example, one East Coast press opened their submissions at midnight and received 300 submissions in six hours, so when the poets on the West Coast were waking up to submit, the call for submissions was already closed.

While these open submission calls are often free, some will require a reading fee anywhere from $5 to $35. Sometimes a press will have a small reading fee just to ensure you are serious about your writing. This prevents the press from being overrun with submissions that do not follow the guidelines and discourages those that lack quality and professionalism. Be sure to read the guidelines for these open submissions carefully because presses ask for different things.

When you submit your work to presses, do so professionally. As an author, you want to connect with the press in the best way possible. If you submit your work and you realize you have a spelling error in your manuscript, leave it be, do not contact them. Presses understand manuscripts are not perfect—that's their job to help you find the errors.

If the press you are submitting to wants a cover letter with your manuscript, address the cover letter to the editor(s) or poetry editor(s), add your contact info, and a short bio. If your manuscript has been a finalist or semi-finalist in other poetry prizes, this is an excellent place to share that information. You can also include one-sentence about your manuscript or a short paragraph of explanation if you like, but for most presses, that isn't necessary.

What Would Walt Whitman Do?

If you would like to bypass presses altogether, consider self-publishing.

Some poets have one goal—to have a book. They don't care who publishes it, where it's available, or if it has a publicity department backing it—they just want a print book with their name on it. Some want to give it to friends and family, and some want to have a book to sell at readings. We are in a time where you can self-publish on your own through various self-publishing platforms such as Kindle Direct, Ingram, Smashmouth, Lulu, and others.

The positive aspect of self-publication is that you control everything. From cover art to font choice, you are creating the book you want to put out in the world. You can add images or do whatever you would like. It's your book and you're in charge.

The negative aspect of self-publication is that you control everything. All work falls on you. The challenge of self-publication is that you have to do (or hire someone to do) all the work—including formatting your poems on the page, creating a table of contents, an acknowledgment page, designing a cover, buying an ISBN number, and more—all while making sure the book is error-free. Also, the book will only get into bookstores through your own effort.

There are many detailed articles online where you can learn more about how to self-publish a book (and there are also many self-published books on how to as well!). So if this sounds like the best way for you, a quick internet search on "how to self-publish a poetry book" will give you some ways and details to begin.

In the end, each poet is on their own journey and needs to decide for themselves how they want to publish their book. It's in your best interest to determine why you want to publish a book of poems and the best path. And it doesn't have to be an either/or decision. Perhaps you want to try entering contests and open submissions for several years, then decide to self-publish. There is no one right way to get a book of poems published and unfortunately, there is no secret handshake either. But understanding your motivations and determining your own best course to publication will help pave your way, along with a well-crafted manuscript built of strong poems with a great title and a poet behind it who professionally follows guidelines—that will take you far.

The Art of the Blurb

~Kimberly L. Becker

blurb (n.)
used by U.S. scholar Brander Matthews in 1906 in "American
Character;" popularized 1907 by U.S. humorist Frank Gelett
Burgess. Originally mocking excessive praise printed on book
jackets, and probably derisively imitative.

So your book is going to be published: congratulations! Along with reading galley proofs, now comes the sometimes dreaded, but often exciting, step of procuring blurbs—those endorsements of your work that will go on the back cover and entice curious readers to buy your book as they browse book fairs, tables at readings, or maybe even actual bookstores. (Remember those?) I have been acquainted with the blurb. I have been both blurber and blurbee. A few field notes:

Whom to ask?

It can be someone with whom you already have a connection or someone whose work you admire from afar. Don't be afraid to ask, but be respectful of the time it entails. Have confidence, but have humility.

Other poets are usually receptive, but don't send your manuscript before asking. If the person is receptive, you may suggest a timeline (based on your publisher's needs), but don't demand; try to be flexible and accommodating, as anyone who blurbs your book is doing so out of generosity and it will take time away from that poet's own work.

If someone agrees to blurb, but doesn't follow through, let it go. Maybe send one email to inquire if the poet has had a chance to consider offering a blurb, but don't hound him or her. It takes time and energy to read a manuscript carefully enough to write a blub and sometimes life intervenes.

How long should a blurb be?

150 words is a good length, long enough to be substantive, but short enough to be read quickly. Confession: as blurber, I sometimes have difficulty writing a short endorsement; in fact one of my blurbs became the foreword to Marc Vincenz's *Beautiful Rush* (Unlikely Books) and one for Malaika King Albrecht's forthcoming *The Stumble Fields* (Main Street Rag) may end up as the preface or as a review. If someone writes you a long blurb, rejoice: you can use excerpts for a short blurb, while retaining the rest for a review or preface. But in general, concision is best.

If you get turned down, thank the poet and move on. Understand that some writers are simply too busy or too much in demand to accommodate every request. It takes vulnerability to ask, but as with any submission, be prepared that you might be rejected or not get your first choice.

As blurber, I have never said no, but then again, I am not a famous poet being asked from all quarters.

As blurbee, I have been honored that everyone whom I have asked has said yes, and only once did a yes not convert to an actual blurb, but since I had asked several people, that was not an issue and I do not take it personally. As poets, we are professional writers and as such, we are better off investing our energy in writing and publishing well, rather than imagining slights.

How many people to ask?

Ask for more than you think you need in case someone is not able to follow through. My publishers have recommended three at a minimum and four or five to have a wider range of opinions and options. Your publisher can also provide you with suggestions. For those of us writing outside academia, especially, it helps to cultivate a social media presence to stay in touch with other poets. Creating an online community allows you to support other writers, who will in turn, be more likely to support you.

From the perspective of the blurber, I have always felt privileged when a poet asks me to blurb his or her work. I enjoy the process of delving into a manuscript, looking for connections and the challenge of how to condense the poet's vision into a description that will draw in other readers.

Therein lies the tension: **the blurb is an act of appreciation, but it is also a marketing tool**. It needs to not be fake and smarmy, but rather insightful and honest. As blurber, if you cannot say anything good about someone's work after reading the manuscript then it is best for everyone if you just say that you do not feel you're the best match. If as blurbee, someone tells you this, then simply thank that poet and trust that another poet will be a better fit for your work.

The blurb is part literary transaction and necessity for publication and part community service. As poets we so often work in isolation that having someone blurb our book creates a sense of literary community.

If you are the blurber, your name is going on that book for all time, so take it seriously.

If you are the blurbee, the names of other poets are going to be associated with your work for as long as copies of your book are floating around, so choose your prospective blurbers carefully, but do not overthink it. You already know poets whose work you read and admire, even if you have not met them in person, so take a risk and ask; the worst they can say is no.

It is a great feeling to be read and understood and it is a great privilege to read and seek to understand such that other readers might be led to read and appreciate another poet's work. For me writing a blurb or asking for a blurb very often results in several exchanged messages of support and the joy of feeling heard or making another poet feel heard. That is a gift.

If publication is, as Cynthia Ozick described it (in her *Paris Review* Interview on the Art of Fiction) the first consummation and being read is the second consummation, then **the blurb helps secure that second consummation**. Blurbs show that other poets esteem your work. As blurber, it is a privilege to be one of the first allowed to read a manuscript. As blurbee, it is a moment of joy (and sometimes tears) to feel your work has been read and appreciated by someone whose caliber of work you aspire to.

Yes, the word *blurb* is unfortunately comical and certainly could devolve into faint praise or purple prose. But if you choose your blurbers wisely, you will have **early praise** that amplifies your book's message and adds to your cachet as a poet.

And when you are fortunate to be asked to blurb, do so with the same humility as when you first asked for a blurb. Because as poets, we are not in competition. We are poets who read and support the work of other poets. **The blurb is one way we fulfill our literary bonds** rather than indulging in what Lewis Hyde (in *The Gift: Imagination and the Erotic Life of Property*) called "a solitary egoism."

The humble blurb connects us as poets.
The blurb humbles us even as it strokes our ego.
The blurb mediates between poet and reader.
The blurb, though required by publisher, is gifted from poet to poet.

A blurb by any other name would, well, you know the rest.

IV. Resources and Ideas

Everyone's process is different—I didn't set out with a vision for a book as a whole, but by allowing myself to write whatever was important to me, the poems came together to express a vision. I took a chance and asked (for a first book) an outside person unfamiliar with my work to help clarify themes and arrange them in a way that allowed them to have interesting conversations with each other.

~Jennifer Markell, *Singing at High Altitude*

The Cover Art Conundrum: What's Best for Your Book?

~Susan Rich

There are so many aspects of putting a book together that no one ever talks about in MFA programs, or really, anywhere. Once the title is chosen (another conundrum) and the decision on sections or no sections is completed, it's time to look for cover art. Or, this is the way it works for me. Perhaps, for some people, the cover art comes earlier but I need to have a sense of the book as a whole before I can make much progress. Also, while it's true some presses have a book designer on staff, even in these cases, the publisher will be happy to have your input. Do know, however, that the press, and not the poet, have final say.

1. **Covers can sell books.** An alluring cover can create a buzz concerning the contents inside. Alternatively, an unattractive cover can turn readers away. This is what a bookseller friend told me. This is also part of what makes the choosing so hard.

2. **The image needs to interact with words**. In other words, where on the image will your book title and name go? Of course, the image can be isolated and framed away from the title and author, but this limits the graphic design.

3. **Be sure to contact the artist *before* you fall in love.** While searching for cover art for my book, *Cloud Pharmacy*, I found what I believed was the perfect image. Dutch photographer, Berndnaut Smilde, has become increasingly famous for creating and photographing clouds inside open spaces. However, when I wrote asking permission to use his photographs, he responded with a polite no. When I wrote a second time with all the eloquence I could garner, the answer remained the same. This made finding my final image all the harder as I couldn't let go of "my" cloud room.

4. Keep a file of possible cover art. There are several cool ways to do this. If you start a file in PowerPoint, you can easily add your book title and name. Try the text in several fonts and in several different arrangements. This will give you a good sense of how well the image works as a book image. I also started a Pinterest page so that I could keep track of possible artwork.

5. Give yourself plenty of time. Most writers I know choose three or four different book covers before they settle on one. Go to museums, to galleries, to coffee shops that curate local art shows, and get acquainted with the art that pulls you in. Try to determine what elements speak to you. For example, I learned that covers that include motion (a bird flying, a group of feathers falling) are extremely compelling.

6. Visit bookstores, libraries, and your own shelves to determine which book covers pull you in and which do not. This will become second nature to you after a while, like when you're shopping for cars all the models on the road begin to catch your eye.

7. Think outside the box. One classic cover I love is, *And Her Soul Out of Nothing* by Olena Kalytiak Davis. The body of a naked woman, her back to the viewer, floats in white space. The image is startling and fits the contents of the poems wonderfully.

8. Don't be too literal. For my second book, *Cures Include Travel,* I chose an image of airmail letters floating in space. The sense of travel came across in the aerogrammes and foreign stamps. For *Cloud Pharmacy* I began by looking at images of apothecary bottles and old pharmacies, but ultimately, I wanted something that brought an extra layer of meaning to the poems.

9. Artwork alone does not a cover make. For *Cloud Pharmacy*, I worked closely with the designer at White Pine Press to find a font I liked and to place the title within the image. These decisions are essential to the overall look of the book.

10. Remember, there are several superb ways to represent your work visually. At different times I had over a dozen works of art that I was seriously considering for *Cloud Pharmacy*. These included everything from apothecary bottles, to floating clouds, to a woman in a boat. The list goes on. Finally, there were several different representations for the work and no one ultimate star.

11. Try to enjoy the process. This is your book! Your love child! Yes, it's nerve wracking but it is also a wonderful gift. You will have a book in the world, and you will get to choose which slinky black dress or favorite blue jeans its dressed in. Let your book be something that "feels" like you.

Try This for Cover Art:

1. Go to websites of your favorite poetry publishers and browse their covers to get ideas about what is beautiful to you.

2. Start a Pinterest page of images that could work for your cover art.

3. Search for copyright-free and/or royalty-free images.

4. Are any of your friends visual artists? See if they have a piece of artwork you could use or consider commissioning a piece by them.

Finding the Publisher That Is Right for You

~Kelli Russell Agodon

Make a list of 10 or more presses you'd be interested in having your book published by. Once you have your list, go on the internet and find their websites:

- Look at their new covers and authors. Are these covers which you like? Authors you'd want to be associated with?
- Do they have any upcoming contests or open submission periods?
- How can you buy their books? Are they available on their website? On Amazon?
- Do they have an active social media presence? Is that Something you care about or not?
- Make a list of all the things you like about them, the things you don't like, and any questions or uncertainties.
- If they are a press that will go on your "to submit to" list, maybe buy a book from them.
- Go to their "About" page and learn who their editors are.
- Do an online search to find interviews with their editors or google the press using the Google filter "news." See what has been written about them.
- Go to their social media pages to learn more about them, what they are promoting, what they are putting out into the world, and who they are.

Look at all of the presses you wrote down, and put a star by your top presses, and write down any times they are open for submissions through contests or open submission periods.

Continue to add to this list as you run across new books of poems and poets. Maybe each evening, research one new press. Allow your list to grow, and remember to focus on what you are looking for in a press. One person may think a big press would be perfect for them, but someone else would feel overwhelmed and disconnected in that environment.

Again, there is no wrong press—just presses that will be able to fit your needs as a poet, and the main way to determine that is to continue to research them and buy books.

Note: if there are no bookstores in your area, maybe go online and check out what has recently been published. Poetry Daily has a good list of new books received in their Hot Off the Presses section. This list also includes an image of each book.

Different Ways to Order Your Poems: A Cheat Sheet

~Susan Rich

1. **Create a chronology.** For example: the story of a young woman as a Dominican nun, the woman leaving the convent, and eventually marrying and creating a family of her own. This is the narrative arc of Annette Spaulding-Convy's book, *In the Convent We Become Clouds*.

2. **Use a braiding approach.** Once you know the themes of your book you can work your poems into a balanced mix of those themes. This allows for different poems to breathe more freely and talk to the other poems. Look at Rick Barot's book, *Chord*.

3. **Notecard surprise.** See Lola Haskins helpful non-fiction book, *Not Feathers Yet*. Keep each poem on a notecard. Write down the title, first line, and last line of each poem. Improvise different colors for each section of your book; there are endless ways to use your manuscript deck of cards.

4. **Emotional arc.** Perhaps the movement is from the exterior world into the interior life of the speaker. Natasha Tretheway's *Belloq's Ophelia* works this way.

5. **Incantation / Transformation / Song.** These are the section titles of my third book, *The Alchemist's Kitchen* and honestly these echo the movement in each of my first three books: a beginning, middle, and (I hope) a satisfying end. Each section uses a braided approach but the strategy could be chronological, too.

6. **Unifying Overarching Theme / Project.** This is important to publishers; the poems need to cohere. A clear theme/concept needs to emerge. Needs glue. In Cindy Veach's collection, *Her Kind*, the poems examine the idea of women construed as witch both in the time of the Salem witch trials and now, in the 21st century.

7. **Mirroring Approach**. Claudia Emerson's *Late Wife* comes to mind here. The poems start out about the speaker's divorce and by the end of the collection she has become the "late" wife of a second man who is a widower. *Late Wife* has many different resonances throughout the book.

Sample Cover Letter

Milkweed Editions
1011 Washington Avenue South
Open Book, Suite 300
Minneapolis, MN 55415

Dear Poetry Reader:

Thank you for offering open submission for poetry manuscripts at Milkweed Editions! I am enclosing mine, entitled *xxxs,* for your consideration.

Though I have not yet published a book, more than three-fourths of these poems have appeared in regional and national poetry journals, including *Poetry, Poetry Daily, The Iowa Review, The Southern Review, Prairie Schooner, Mid-American Review,* and many other publications, mostly within the last three years. A version of this manuscript has been a finalist three times in the last year in various poetry competitions. I was awarded a 2005 Poetry Fellowship from the National Endowment of the Arts based on portions of this manuscript, and since 2002 I have received other regional fellowships and awards. I teach poetry in the schools through the Washington State Arts Commission and through Writers in the Schools in Seattle. I am also one of the editors and president of Floating Bridge Press, a non-profit press dedicated to publishing Washington State poets.

Something I do not ordinarily include in my official biography is the fact I came to poetry in my thirties, am now in my forties. I think my poems demonstrate a mature—that is, conflicted, uneasy—outlook. They arise out of daily life: parenting three children, watching friends struggle, losing my parents, trying to understand my marriage.

I have been a fan of Milkweed Editions since I read Jim Moore's beautiful and profound book, *The Long Experience of Love*, about seven years ago. I hope you will find my work is compatible in style to the fine work you have already published. I'm a true admirer of your press.

If you need to reach me, please call me at (206)___ or write to___. Thank you for this opportunity to submit my work, and for your consideration.

Sincerely,

Soon-to-be-famous-poet

Contributor Notes

Before my book was taken, I tossed 2-3 previous manuscripts. I paid two professional editors and sent the book out for 2 + years. I received 47 rejections. During that time, I radically revised the manuscript multiple times. Eventually, in an oddly beautiful twist, a Quaker press took it. The book is very, er, intimate and also highlights struggles with Christianity, so I almost didn't send it to that press. And yet.. and yet....

~Lauren Davis. *Home Beneath the Church*

Lana Hechtman Ayers has shepherded over a hundred poetry volumes into print in her role as managing editor at three small presses. She lives on the Oregon coast in a town known for its barking sea lions. Lana's work appears in *Escape Into Life, Rattle, The London Reader, Peregrine, The MacGuffin*, and other journals. Her latest poetry collections are: *When All Else Fails* (The Poetry Box, 2023) and *Overtures* (Kelsay Books, 2023). Visit her at: www.LanaAyers.com.

Sandra Beasley is the author of four poetry collections—*Made to Explode, Count the Waves, I Was the Jukebox*, which won the 2009 Barnard Women Poets Prize, and *Theories of Falling*—as well as *Don't Kill the Birthday Girl: Tales from an Allergic Life*, a disability memoir and cultural history of food allergies. She served as the editor for *Vinegar and Char: Verse from the Southern Foodways Alliance*. Honors for her work include the 2019 Munster Literature Centre's John Montague International Poetry Fellowship, a 2015 NEA fellowship, and six DC Commission on the Arts and Humanities fellowships. She lives in Washington, D.C.

Of mixed descent, including Cherokee, **Kimberly L. Becker** is the author of *Words Facing East* and *The Dividings* (WordTech Editions), *The Bed Book and Bringing Back the Fire* (Spuyten Duyvil), and *Flight* (MadHat Press). Her work appears widely, including *Indigenous Message on Water; Tending the Fire: Native Voices and Portraits,* and forthcoming in *Unpapered*. Nominated for a Pushcart, she has read at Busboys and Poets, The National Museum of the American Indian (Washington, DC), Split This Rock, and Wordfest. She has served as a mentor for PEN America's Prison Writing and AWP's Writer-to-Writer programs. She lives in North Dakota. www.kimberlylbecker.com

Kristin Berkey-Abbott earned a Ph.D. in English from the University of South Carolina. She has taught at many colleges, and while she still continues to teach, she is also pursuing a Master of Divinity degree from Wesley Theological Seminary. She has published three chapbooks: *Whistling Past the Graveyard* (Pudding House Publications), *I Stand Here Shredding Documents*, and *Life in the Holocene Extinction* (both published by Finishing Line Press).

Nickole Brown is the author of *Sister* and *Fanny Says*. She lives in Asheville, NC, where she volunteers at several animal sanctuaries. *To Those Who Were Our First Gods*, a chapbook of poems about these animals, won the 2018 Rattle Prize, and her essay-in-poems, *The Donkey Elegies*, was published by Sibling Rivalry Press in 2020. In 2021, Spruce Books of Penguin Random House published *Write It! 100 Poetry Prompts to Inspire*, a book she co-authored with her wife, Jessica Jacobs; they regularly teach generative writing sessions together as part of their SunJune Literary Collaborative. She is also on faculty at the Sewanee School of Letters MFA Program.

Gloria J. McEwen Burgess's poetry celebrates the rich oral traditions of her ancestors—African, Scots Irish, and Native American. Her poetry appears in diverse anthologies, including *The Ringing Ear: Black Poets Lean South* and *Gathering Ground: A Reader Celebrating Cave Canem's First Decade*. Her books of poetry include *The Open Door* and *Journey of the Rose*. She has also written a visual biography, *Pass It On!*, about her father's life-changing relationship with Nobel Laureate William Faulkner. Dr. Burgess hails from Mississippi and lives in North Carolina.

Lauren Camp is the Poet Laureate of New Mexico and the author of five books, most recently *Took House* (Tupelo Press). Two new books—*Worn Smooth Between Devourings* (NYQ Books) and *An Eye in Each Square* (River River Books)—are forthcoming in 2023. Honors include a Dorset Prize and finalist citations for the Arab American Book Award and Adrienne Rich Award for Poetry. Her poems have appeared in *Kenyon Review, Prairie Schooner, Beloit Poetry Journal, Missouri Review,* and *Poet Lore*, and her work has been translated into Mandarin, Turkish, Spanish, and Arabic. www.laurencamp.com

Kelly Davio is the author of the poetry collections *Burn This House* (Red Hen Press, 2013) and *The Book of the Unreal Woman* (Broken Sleep Books, 2022), as well as the essay collection *It's Just Nerves* (Squares and Rebels, 2017). She is a former editor of *The Los Angeles Review* and founding editor of Tahoma Literary Review.

Oliver de la Paz is the Poet Laureate of Worcester, MA for 2023-2025. He is the author and editor of seven books: *Names Above Houses,*

Furious Lullaby, Requiem for the Orchard, Post Subject: A Fable, and *The Boy in the Labyrinth,* a finalist for the Massachusetts Book Award in Poetry. His newest work, *The Diaspora Sonnets,* is forthcoming from Liveright Press in 2023. He teaches at the College of the Holy Cross and in the Low-Residency MFA Program at Pacific Lutheran University.

Risa Denenberg lives on the Olympic Peninsula in Washington State where she works as a nurse practitioner. She is a cofounder of Headmistress Press; curator at *The Poetry Café Online*; and an avid book reviewer. Her most recent publications include the full-length collection, *slight faith* (MoonPath Press, 2018), and the chapbook, *Posthuman*, finalist in the Floating Bridge 2020 chapbook competition. https://risadenenberg.com

Jose Hernandez Diaz is a 2017 NEA Poetry Fellow. He is the author of *The Parachutist* (Texas Review Press, 2023) and the chapbook: *The Fire Eater* (Texas Review Press, 2020). His work appears in *The American Poetry Review, Boulevard, Colorado Review, Georgia Review, Iowa Review, The Missouri Review, Poetry, The Southern Review, The Yale Review,* and *The Best American Nonrequired Reading Anthology*. He teaches creative writing online and edits for Frontier Poetry.

Saddiq Dzukogi is the author of *Your Crib, My Qibla* (University of Nebraska Press, 2021) winner of the Derek Walcott Prize for Poetry and the Julie Suk Award, as well as a finalist of the Nigeria Prize for Literature. He is an Assistant Professor of English at Mississippi State University.

Jennifer Givhan is a Mexican-American poet, novelist, and transformational coach from the Southwestern desert who's earned fellowships from the National Endowment for the Arts and PEN Emerging Voices. The author of five full-length poetry collections (most recently *Belly to the Brutal* forthcoming this year from Wesleyan University Press) and the novels *Trinity Sight, Jubilee, and River Woman River Demon*, her work has appeared in T*he New Republic, The Nation, POETRY* and many others. Follow her at jennifergivhan.com.

Diana Goetsch is the author of eight collections of poems, including *Nameless Boy* (2015) and *In America* (2017), and a memoir, *This Body I Wore* (FSG, 2022). Her work has appeared in leading journals and anthologies, including *The New Yorker, Poetry, Gettysburg Review, The Iowa Review, LitHub, The American Scholar, The Pushcart Prize, Best American Poetry*. Goetsch is a recipient of fellowships from the National Endowment for the Arts, the New York Foundation for the Arts, and The New School, where she was the 2017 Grace Paley Teaching Fellow. She resides in New York City.

Lee Herrick is the California Poet Laureate. He is the author of three books of poems: *Scar and Flower, Gardening Secrets of the Dead*, and *This Many Miles from Desire,* and co-editor of *The World I Leave You: Asian American Poets on Faith and Spirit*. He served as Fresno Poet Laureate from 2015-2017. Born in Daejeon, Korea, and adopted to the United States at ten months, he teaches at Fresno City College and the MFA program at the University of Nevada Reno at Lake Tahoe.

Su Hwang is a poet, activist, stargazer, and the author of *Bodega* (Milkweed Editions), which received the 2020 Minnesota Book Award in poetry and was named a finalist for the 2021 Kate Tufts Discovery Award. Born in Seoul, Korea, she was raised in New York then called the Bay Area home before transplanting to the Midwest. A recipient of the inaugural Jerome Hill Fellowship in Literature, she is a teaching artist with the Minnesota Prison Writing Workshop, and is the cofounder with poet Sun Yung Shin, of Poetry Asylum.

Jennifer Jean's poetry collections include *VOZ, Object Lesson*, and *The Fool*. Her teaching resource book is *Object Lesson: a Guide to Writing Poetry*. She's received honors, residencies, and fellowships from the Kenyon Review Writers Workshop, DISQUIET/Dzanc Books, the Massachusetts Cultural Council, the Her Story Is collective, the Academy of American Poets, and the Women's Federation for World Peace. As well, her poems and co-translations have appeared in *POETRY, Rattle, The Common, Waxwing, On the Seawall*, and elsewhere. Jennifer edits translations for Consequence Forum and is the senior program manager of 24PearlStreet, the Fine Arts Work Center's online writing program.

Kirun Kapur is the author of *Women in the Waiting Room* (Black Lawrence Press, 2020), a finalist for the National Poetry Series, the Julie Suk Award and the Massachusetts Book Award. Her first book, *Visiting Indira Gandhi's Palmist* (Elixir Press, 2015) won the Arts & Letters Rumi Prize and the Antivenom Poetry Award. She serves as editor at the *Beloit Poetry Journal* and teaches at Amherst College, where she is director of the Creative Writing Program.

Tina Kelley's *Rise Wildly* appeared in 2020 from CavanKerry Press, joining *Abloom & Awry, Precise,* and *The Gospel of Galore*, a Washington State Book Award winner. She co-authored *Breaking Barriers: How P-TECH Schools Create a Pathway from High School to College to Career* and *Almost Home: Helping Kids Move from Homelessness to Hope* and reported for a decade for *The New York Times*. Her poems have appeared in *Poetry East, Southwest Review, Prairie Schooner,* and *The Best American Poetry 2009*. She's the senior education reporter for NJ.com. She and her husband have two children and live in Maplewood, NJ.

Anna Leahy's latest books are the poetry collections *What Happened Was,* and *Aperture,* and the nonfiction book *Tumor*. Her poetry has appeared at *Atlanta Review, Bennington Review, Poetry, Scientific American,* and elsewhere, and her essays won top awards from *Mississippi Review, Los Angeles Review, Ninth Letter,* and *Dogwood*. She edits the international *Tab Journal* and has been a fellow at MacDowell and the American Library in Paris. She directs the MFA in Creative Writing and co-directs the Health Humanities program at Chapman University. More at https://amleahy.com or on Twitter @AMLeahy.

Claudia Castro Luna is the author of *Cipota Under the Moon* (Tia Chucha Press, 2022); *One River, A Thousand Voices* (Chin Music Press, 2020 & 2022); *Killing Marías* (Two Sylvias, 2017), and the chapbook *This City* (Floating Bridge, 2016). She served as Washington's State Poet Laureate (2018 – 2021) and as Seattle's inaugural Civic Poet (2015-2017). She was named Academy of American Poets Laureate Fellow in 2019. Her most recent nonfiction is in *There's a Revolution Outside, My Love: Letters from a Crisis* (Vintage). Born in El Salvador, Castro Luna came to the United States in 1981. Living in English and Spanish, she writes and teaches in Seattle on unceded Duwamish territory.

Dennis Maloney is a poet and translator. A number of volumes of his own poetry have been published including *Just Enough, Listening to Tao Yuan Ming, The Things I Notice Now*, and *The Faces of Guan Yin*. A bilingual German/English volume, Empty Cup was published in Germany in 2017. His most recent collection is *Windows*. He is also the editor and publisher of the widely respected White Pine Press in Buffalo, NY.

Jennifer Martelli is the author of *The Queen of Queens* (Bordighera Press) and *My Tarantella* (Bordighera Press), named a "Must Read" by the Massachusetts Center for the Book, and awarded Finalist for the Housatonic Book Award. Martelli's chapbooks include *After Bird* (Grey Book Press) and *In the Year of Ferraro* (Nixes Mate). Her work has appeared in *Poetry, The Academy of American Poets Poem-a-Day, The Tahoma Literary Review, Thrush, Cream City Review, The Shore, River Mouth Review,* and elsewhere. Jennifer Martelli has twice received grants for poetry from the Massachusetts Cultural Council. She is co-poetry editor for *Mom Egg Review.*

January Gill O'Neil is an associate professor at Salem State University, and the author of *Rewilding* (2018), *Misery Islands* (2014), and *Underlife* (2009), all published by CavanKerry Press. From 2012-2018, she served as the executive director of the Massachusetts Poetry Festival, and currently serves on the boards of AWP and Montserrat College of Art. Her poems and articles have appeared in *The New York Times Magazine*, the Academy of American Poets' Poem-A-Day series, *American Poetry Review, Green Mountains Review, Poetry*, and *Sierra* magazine, among others. Her poem, "At the Rededication of the Emmett Till Memorial," was a co-winner of the 2022 Allen Ginsberg Poetry award from the Poetry Center at Passaic County Community College. The recipient of fellowships from the Massachusetts Cultural Council, Cave Canem, and the Barbara Deming Memorial Fund, O'Neil was the 2019-2020 John and Renée Grisham Writer-in-Residence at the University of Mississippi, Oxford. O'Neil is one of five judges for the 2022 National Book Award in poetry. She lives with her two children in Beverly, MA.

April Ossmann is the author of *Event Boundaries* and *Anxious Music* (Four Way Books) and *We* (Red Hen Press, 2025), recipient of a Vermont Arts Council Creation Grant, and former executive director of Alice James Books. She is an independent editor (poetry, essays, reviews): www.aprilossmann.com ; and was a faculty editor for the low-residency MFA in Creative Writing Program at Sierra Nevada College.

Linda Pastan (1932-2023) was born in New York City, but lived most of her life in Maryland, where she was that state's poet laureate. She was a winner of the prestigious Ruth Lily Poetry prize and was twice a finalist for the National Book Award. She was the author of *Almost An Elegy: New and Later Selected Poems* (W.W. Norton, 2022), *Insomnia* (W. W. Norton, 2015); *Traveling Light* (W. W. Norton, 2011); *Queen of a Rainy Country* (W. W. Norton, 2006); *The Last Uncle* (W. W. Norton, 2002); *Carnival Evening: New and Selected Poems 1968-1998* (W. W. Norton, 1998), which was nominated for the National Book Award; *An Early Afterlife* (W. W. Norton, 1995); *Heroes In Disguise* (W. W. Norton, 1991), *The Imperfect Paradise* (W. W. Norton, 1988), a nominee for the Los Angeles Times Book Prize; *PM/AM: New and Selected Poems* (W. W. Norton, 1982), which was nominated for the National Book Award; *The Five Stages of Grief* (W. W. Norton, 1978), and *A Perfect Circle of Sun* (Swallow Press, 1971).

Alison Pelegrin is an NEA fellow and the author of four poetry collections, most recently *Our Lady of Bewilderment* (LSU Press 2022). She is writer-in-residence at Southeastern Louisiana University.

Michelle Peñaloza is the author of Former Possessions of the Spanish Empire, winner of the 2018 Hillary Gravendyk National Poetry Prize (Inlandia Books, 2019). She is also the author of two chapbooks, *landscape/heartbreak* (Two Sylvias, 2015), and *Last Night I Dreamt of Volcanoes* (Organic Weapon Arts, 2015). The recipient of fellowships and awards from the University of Oregon and Kundiman, Michelle has also received support from Caldera, Willapa Bay AIR, VONA/Voices, and the Bread Loaf Writers' Conference, among others. The proud daughter of Filipino immigrants, Michelle was born in the suburbs of Detroit, MI and raised in Nashville, TN. She now lives in rural Northern California.

Jessy Randall's poems, comics, and other things have appeared in *McSweeney's, Poetry,* and *Scientific American.* Her most recent book is *Mathematics for Ladies: Poems on Women in Science* (Gold SF, 2022). She also co-authored two collections of poetry: *Interruptions* (Pecan Grove Press, 2011) and *What If You Were Happy for Just One Second* (BOAAT, 2014) with Daniel M. Shapiro. She is the Curator of Special Collections at Colorado College, and her website is http://bit.ly/JessyRandall

In 2003, **Spencer Reece** authored *The Clerk's Tale*, selected by Louise Glück, was awarded the Bakeless Prize. In 2014, *The Road to Emmaus* was published, long-listed for the National Book Award, and short-listed for the Griffin Prize. In 2017, Reece edited a bilingual anthology of poems by the abandoned girls of Our Little Roses, *Counting Time Like People Count Stars.* In 2021, two new works appeared, nonfiction and watercolors—*The Secret Gospel of Mark: A Poet's Memoir* and *All The Beauty Still Left: A Poet's Painted Book of Hours.* An Episciopal priest, he has served in San Pedro Sula, Honduras; Madrid, Spain; and New York City, New York. Reese is currently the vicar of St. Paul's, Wickford, Rhode Island. A decade in the making, *Acts* is his third collection of poems.

Greg Santos is a poet, editor, and educator. He holds an MFA in Creative Writing from The New School. He is the author of *Ghost Face* and several other poetry collections. He is an adoptee of Cambodian, Spanish, and Portuguese heritage. He lives in Montreal with his family.

Daniel M. Shapiro is a special education teacher who lives in Pittsburgh. *Interruptions*, his full-length collaboration with Jessy Randall, has become a collector's item. His solo books of poems include *(This Is Not) A Mixtape for the End of the World, How the Potato Chip Was Invented*, and *Heavy Metal Fairy Tales.*

Diane Seuss is the author of five books of poetry, including *frank: sonnets* (Graywolf Press, 2021), winner of the 2022 PEN/Voelcker Award for Poetry, the 2021 National Book Critics Circle Award for Poetry, and the 2022 Pulitzer Prize for Poetry; *Still Life with Two Dead Peacocks and a Girl* (Graywolf Press, 2018), a finalist for the National Book Critics Circle Award in Poetry and the Los Angeles Times Book

Prize in Poetry; *Four-Legged Girl* (Graywolf Press, 2015), a finalist for the Pulitzer Prize; and *Wolf Lake, White Gown Blown Open* (University of Massachusetts Press, 2010), recipient of the Juniper Prize for Poetry. A Guggenheim fellow, Seuss was writer-in-residence at Kalamazoo College for many years, and has been a visiting professor at Colorado College, the University of Michigan's Helen Zell Writers' Program, and Washington University in St. Louis.

Michael Schmeltzer is a biracial author originally from Japan. He currently lives in Seattle where he serves as Editor-in-Chief of Floating Bridge Press. His most recent book of poems, *Empire of Surrender,* is the winner of the Wandering Aengus Book Award. Along with writer Meghan McClure, he is the co-author of the nonfiction book *A Single Throat Opens*, a lyric exploration of addiction and family. His debut full-length *Blood Song* was a finalist for the Washington State Book Award in Poetry, the Julie Suk Award, and the Coil Book Award. His honors include a Jack Straw Fellowship, the Gulf Stream Award for Poetry, and *Blue Earth Review's* Flash Fiction Prize.

Jeff Shotts is Executive Editor and Director of Poetry at Graywolf Press, where he acquires and edits works of poetry, essay, lyric nonfiction, and translation. In 2017, he received the Editor's Award from Poets & Writers. He lives in Minneapolis, Minnesota.

Maggie Smith is the bestselling author of several books of poetry and prose, including *Goldenrod, Good Bones, Keep Moving*, and *You Could Make This Place Beautiful* (Atria/Simon & Schuster, 2023). Smith's poems and essays have appeared in the *New York Times, The New Yorker*, the *Guardian*, the *Paris Review*, *Tin House*, the *Washington Post*, and *The Best American Poetry*.

Susan Terris is a freelance editor and the author of 7 poetry books—mostly Omnidawn and Marsh Hawk—seven chapbooks, three artist's books, two plays. Journals include *The Southern Review, Georgia Review, Prairie Schooner, Blackbird,* and *Ploughshares*. She has had poems published both in *Pushcart Prize* and in *Best American Poetry.* www.susanterris.com

Melissa Studdard is the author of the poetry collections, *Dear Selection Committee* and *I Ate the Cosmos for Breakfast*, as well as the chapbook *Like a Bird with a Thousand Wings*. Her work has been featured by PBS, NPR, *The New York Times, The Guardian, Ms. Magazine,* and the Academy of American Poets' Poem-a-Day series, and has appeared in periodicals such as *POETRY, Kenyon Review,* and *New England Review.* Her Awards include the Lucille Medwick Memorial Award from the Poetry Society of America, The Penn Review Poetry Prize, the Tom Howard Prize from Winning Writers, the REELpoetry International Film Festival Audience Choice Award, and more. You can find her at www.melissastuddard.com.

Cindy Veach is the author of *Her Kind* (CavanKerry Press) a finalist for the 2022 Eric Hoffer Montaigne Medal, *Gloved Against Blood* (CavanKerry Press), a finalist for the Paterson Poetry Prize and a Massachusetts Center for the Book 'Must Read,' and the chapbook, *Innocents* (Nixes Mate). Her poems have appeared in the Academy of American Poets Poem-a-Day, *AGNI, Michigan Quarterly Review, Poet Lore,* and *Salamander* among others. Cindy is the recipient of the Philip Booth Poetry Prize and the Samuel Allen Washington Prize. She is co-poetry editor of MER (*Mom Egg Review*). www.cindyveach.com

Vivian Wagner is the author of a memoir, *Fiddle: One Woman, Four Strings*, and *8,000 Miles of Music* (Citadel-Kensington); a full-length poetry collection, *Raising* (Clare Songbirds Publishing House); and five poetry chapbooks: *The Village* (Aldrich Press-Kelsay Books), *Making* (Origami Poems Project), *Curiosities* (Unsolicited Press), *Spells of the Apocalypse* (Thirty West Publishing House), and *Birch Songs* (Origami Poems Project).

Corrie Williamson is the author of two books of poetry, *The River Where You Forgot My Name* (SIU Press 2019) and *Sweet Husk* (Perugia Press 2014). Her work has appeared in *The Kenyon Review, Southern Review, Ecotone, 32 Poems, AGNI,* and many other venues. She lives in Montana.

About the Editors

Susan Rich is the author of five poetry collections including most recently, *Gallery of Postcards and Maps: New and Selected Poems* (Salmon Poetry) with an introduction by Ilya Kaminsky. Her other books include *Cloud Pharmacy, The Alchemist's Kitchen*, named a finalist for the Foreword Prize and the Washington State Book Award, *Cures Include Travel, and The Cartographer's Tongue,* winner of the PEN USA Award and the Peace Corps Writers award. She edited, along with Ilya Kaminsky and Brian Turner, *The Strangest of Theatres: Poets Writing Across Borders* (Poetry Foundation). Rich has received awards and fellowships from the Fulbright Foundation, PEN USA, and *The Times Literary Supplement* (London). Her sixth collection, *Blue Atlas*, will be published by Red Hen Press next year. Susan is cofounder and executive director of Poets on the Coast: A Writing Retreat for Women. www.poetsusanrich.com

Kelli Russell Agodon's newest book *Dialogues with Rising Tides* (Copper Canyon Press) was named a Finalist in the Washington State Book Awards and shortlisted for the Eric Hoffer Book Award Grand Prize in Poetry. She is the cofounder of Two Sylvias Press, where she works as an editor and book cover designer. Agodon's second book, *Letters from the Emily Dickinson Room,* won the Foreword Prize's Book of the Year in Poetry, as well as being a Finalist for the Washington State Book Award, and named one of GoodRead's Top 20 Books of the Year in Poetry. Kelli teaches at the Rainier Writing Workshop, Pacific Lutheran University's low-res MFA program. She lives in a sleepy seaside town in Washington State on traditional lands of the Chimacum, Coast Salish, S'Klallam, and Suquamish people, where she is an avid paddleboarder and birdwatcher. Kelli is currently part of a project between local land trusts and artists to help raise awareness for the preservation of land, ecosystems, and biodiversity called Writing the Land. www.agodon.com / www.twosylviaspress.com

Publications by Two Sylvias Press:

The Daily Poet: Day-By-Day Prompts For Your Writing Practice
by Kelli Russell Agodon and Martha Silano (Print and eBook)

The Daily Poet Companion Journal (Print)

Everything is Writable: 240 Poetry Prompts from Two Sylvias Press
by Kelli Russell Agodon and Annette Spaulding-Convy (Print)

Demystifying the Manuscript
edited by Susan Rich & Kelli Russell Agodon

Fire On Her Tongue: An Anthology of Contemporary Women's Poetry
edited by Kelli Russell Agodon and Annette Spaulding-Convy (Print and
eBook)

The Poet Tarot and Guidebook: A Deck Of Creative Exploration (Print)

The Inspired Poet: Writing Exercises to Spark New Work
by Susan Landgraf (Print)

At Night My Body Waits, Winner of the 2021 Two Sylvias Press
Chapbook Prize by Saúl Hernández (Print)

Nightmares & Miracles, Winner of the 2020 Two Sylvias Press Wilder
Prize by Michelle Bitting (Print)

Hallucinating a Homestead, Winner of the 2020 Two Sylvias Press
Chapbook Prize by Meg E. Griffitts (Print)

Shade of Blue Trees, Finalist 2019 Two Sylvias Press Wilder Prize
by Kelly Cressio-Moeller (Print)

Disappearing Queen, Winner of the 2019 Two Sylvias Press Wilder Prize
by Gail Martin (Print)

Deathbed Sext, Winner of the 2019 Two Sylvias Press Chapbook Prize
by Christopher Salerno (Print)

Crown of Wild, Winner of the 2018 Two Sylvias Press Wilder Prize
by Erica Bodwell (Print)

American Zero, Winner of the 2018 Two Sylvias Press Chapbook Prize
by Stella Wong (Print and eBook)

All Transparent Things Need Thundershirts, Winner of the 2017 Two
Sylvias Press Wilder Prize by Dana Roeser (Print and eBook)

Where The Horse Takes Wing: The Uncollected Poems of Madeline DeFrees edited by Anne McDuffie (Print and eBook)

In The House Of My Father, Winner of the 2017 Two Sylvias Press Chapbook Prize by Hiwot Adilow (Print and eBook)

Box, Winner of the 2017 Two Sylvias Press Poetry Prize by Sue D. Burton (Print and eBook)

Tsigan: The Gypsy Poem (New Edition) by Cecilia Woloch (Print and eBook)

PR For Poets by Jeannine Hall Gailey (Print and eBook)

Appalachians Run Amok, Winner of the 2016 Two Sylvias Press Wilder Prize by Adrian Blevins (Print and eBook)

Pass It On! by Gloria J. McEwen Burgess (Print)

Killing Marias by Claudia Castro Luna (Print and eBook)

The Ego and the Empiricist, Finalist 2016 Two Sylvias Press Chapbook Prize by Derek Mong (Print and eBook)

The Authenticity Experiment by Kate Carroll de Gutes (Print and eBook)

Mytheria, Finalist 2015 Two Sylvias Press Wilder Prize by Molly Tenenbaum (Print and eBook)

Arab in Newsland , Winner of the 2016 Two Sylvias Press Chapbook Prize by Lena Khalaf Tuffaha (Print and eBook)

The Blue Black Wet of Wood, Winner of the 2015 Two Sylvias Press Wilder Prize by Carmen R. Gillespie (Print and eBook)

Fire Girl: Essays on India, America, and the In-Between by Sayantani Dasgupta (Print and eBook)

Blood Song by Michael Schmeltzer (Print and eBook)

Naming The No-Name Woman, Winner of the 2015 Two Sylvias Press Chapbook Prize by Jasmine An (Print and eBook)

Please visit Two Sylvias Press (www.twosylviaspress.com) for information on purchasing our print books, eBooks, writing tools, and for submission guidelines for our annual book prizes.

Made in USA - North Chelmsford, MA
1358683_9781948767187
02.07.2023 1634